Home At Last

493-MCEN

Home At Last

Personal Narratives by Two
Women of Life in a Small
Island Community

Josie Avery and Grace Hall McEntee

Illustrations by Horace M. Barrett

493-MCEN

Library of Congress Number: 2001116760
ISBN #:   Hardcover   0-7388-9965-8
        Softcover   0-7388-9964-X

This book was printed in the United States of America.

To order additional copies of this book, contact:
Xlibris Corporation
1-888-795-4274
www.Xlibris.com
Orders@Xlibris.com

Table of Contents

List of Illustrations

With love, we dedicate these writings to Sara Harrington and Matt McEntee who brought us to Prudence Island.

Josie Avery and Grace Hall McEntee

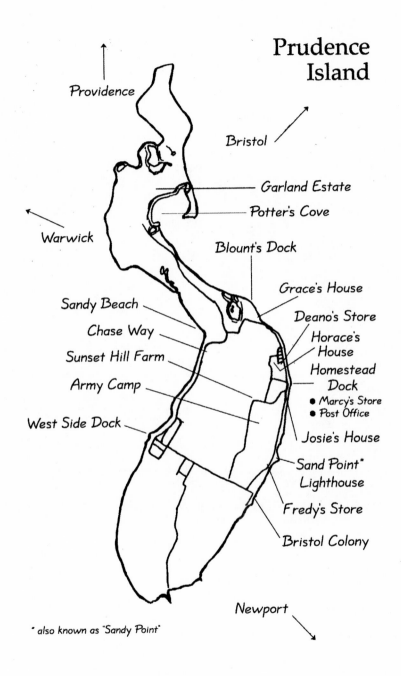

Prudence Island

Providence

Bristol

Garland Estate

Potter's Cove

Blount's Dock

Warwick

Grace's House

Sandy Beach

Deano's Store

Chase Way

Horace's House

Sunset Hill Farm

Homestead Dock

Army Camp

● Marcy's Store
● Post Office

West Side Dock

Josie's House

Sand Point*
Lighthouse

Fredy's Store

Bristol Colony

Newport

* also known as "Sandy Point"

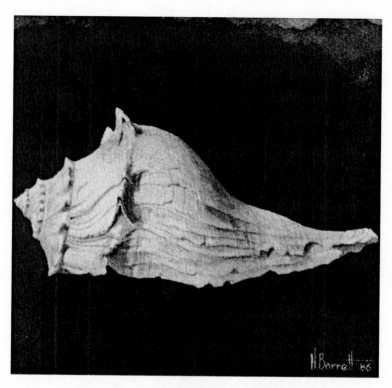

Conch

Introduction

What is it like to live on an island without a bridge? For some, the commute over Narragansett Bay by ferry is a daily reunion with island neighbors. For others of us, piloting a small boat challenges our skills and surprises us with unexpected adventure.

Separation from daily life on the mainland breeds a unique culture. Here on Prudence Island we have our own lingo and our island ways. Our language is sprinkled with references to wind direction, temperature, tides and time.

We savor night walks on the beach, a run on a dirt road, and stopping to talk to a turtle. Kids and adults build relationships, unique friendships that leap barriers that ordinarily separate us from those who might become our friends.

Home At Last emanates from Prudence Island—an island without a bridge—the place where we live.

"Black Slacks and a Nor'easter," "The Rogue Wave,"

"Rock and Roll" and "Time Well Spent" arise from two different styles of commute—island to mainland and back—by ferry and in a twenty-three foot Sea Hawk. "Josie, Sunny Side Up," "Remembering Benny," "Growing Up and Growing Old," "Bob and the Trail Gang" reveal relationships with neighbors and "Soul and Place," "Prudence Island, A Place for Me," and "Home at Last" show relationships with the place where we live.

Like any culture, that of Prudence Island reveals daily life and the forging of traditions. Typical of the culture are stories like "Lost: One Pie," "First Summer," "Glimpses of Island Life," "Planting Peas," "A Place Where Almost Everyone Counts," and "The Family Clambake."

One story emerges from the way a world event played out in a small community and others show how incidents arise from lifestyle. "Gathering Stories, Recording History" illustrates how Prudence Island experienced World War II in its own peculiar way. "The Critter," "A Dead Thing," "*Phragmites* and the Sharp-tailed Sparrow," "Mystery on PI," and "Leave Taking" are about incidents that happened here.

We do not mean to reveal a singular truth that we've known or heard about on Prudence Island, but we intend to show through our writing what it means for two women to live in an island community. We offer our collection of stories to share with you a bit of the island and to connect our lives with yours.

Josie Avery and Grace Hall McEntee

1 | Home at Last

by Josie Avery

After a few summers visiting with the Hudsons and the Harringtons, it was time for the Avery family to buy a place of our own. And so, my parents purchased a small one-bedroom cottage at Homestead. It was a typical island cottage—a galley kitchen with spaces between the floor boards large enough to see the ground below, a combination living and dining area, a bathroom so small my mother said you had to back into it, an outdoor shower, and a porch. Two cots on the screened-in porch—my bedroom for many years—increased the sleeping capacity. Already furnished in the traditional Prudence way of odd castoffs and finds from the dump, it was the ideal cottage for our family.

My mother and brother Scott spent their summers at the cottage, heading down to the island right after school ended and leaving just before Labor Day. In those days every house seemed full of kids and moms who summered on Prudence. Dads would arrive on the Friday evening boats and leave on Sunday evening or Monday morning to go back to work. Daily, the kids would travel from house to house looking for one more kid to go down to the beach for a swim, and the moms watched out for each other's kids. By summer's end, the small neighborhood of families merged into one large communal family.

Over the years my feelings about Prudence changed as my life changed. For a brief period while in high school, I disliked the island. Unhappy to be away from my hometown friends, disliking the damp air which made my curly hair frizz, missing the phone and the television, I rebelled and used every excuse—work, babysitting, a party—not to go to the island. While in college, I rediscovered the island as a place for fun and letting off a little steam. And with the divorce of my parents and later my mother's death, the house on Prudence slowly became a constant in my life—bridging the past to the present and eventually to the future.

Living and working in New York City in the late 1980's, my contact with the island became limited. I arrived every Memorial Day weekend to open up the cottage for the summer rentals—expenses had to be met. At the end of the summer I returned for Labor Day weekend, for a few days respite and to close down the house for the winter months.

One year on the day after Labor Day, I was alone in the cottage. Stepping out the back door, I startled a deer. She ran up the back road into a thicket and thrashed her way through the underbrush. In that moment I had a revelation—I could begin a great adventure. After all the years of coming to Prudence as a sporadic visitor or summer person, I suddenly had a great desire to be closer to the island. Returning to the city, I took all the necessary steps—finding a job, renovating my home—to move to Rhode Island.

In the years before my move to the island, I teased my dad about my plans. Swaddling myself in layers upon layers of winter clothing until only my eyes peeked out, I would walk up to him and say, "Prudence Ferry, February 1st, 6:25 a.m." This would always prompt him to sigh, "Oh, Josie." This less than enthusiastic delivery was his way of expressing the hard life he believed a woman would have on the island.

I only meant to live near Prudence—say in Bristol or Providence—and visit as often as possible. I wanted to be one of those April to October people and maybe board the ferry for an occasional winter weekend. But when I saw my house, I was overcome by its beauty. This was *my* home and so I stayed.

There have been times over the years when the island has suddenly seemed remote and I have thought, "Enough!" At these times, I'll take my dog Molly and go out for long walks on the island. Late at night using the light of the sky or the lights from across the bay, Molly and I walk along Narragansett Avenue near Homestead Dock. During the deserted winter months we may traipse across the yards of silent houses. We listen to the waves lapping at the shore and sniff the air for a sea change. When the moon is near full, we walk along the beach. Sometimes in the dark, we startle a group of deer or they startle us.

As we come along the road, I see the lights of my house and prompt Molly. "Take us home," I say. Molly's pace picks up as she anticipates the warm house and a doggy treat. We walk up the road. Molly bounds ahead and waits for me at home. My home.

2 | Soul and Place

by Grace Hall McEntee

Children inhabit a place. It seeps through their skin, bone, marrow, viscera, and eventually rests within the soul. Soul and place become inseparable.

So it is with any of us who live for a long time, anywhere. So it was with Craig Porter on Prudence Island.

Craig "grew up" in the Bristol Colony section of Prudence Island. A bit of land and a few rocks separated his house from the waters of the East Passage of Narragansett Bay. Growing up on the island meant that he spent as much time on the water as on the land. Recently, I sat with Bill Day, a childhood companion of Craig's, who told me a few stories about Craig and their other friends—Linc Mossop, Allan Beck, and Mike Graham—during the summers of the late 40's and early 50's.

Craig and Bill lived next door to each other. Bill told about one day when Craig and his father were out sailing on a twelve-foot sailboat in front of their houses. They tipped over. A Navy boat that came by and stopped for the rescue used a giant hose to suck all the water out of Craig's boat. By the time they were finished, all the officers and men were soaked. Craig's boat was upright. He and his father sailed away. Craig was ten that summer.

As Craig and his friends were growing up, Todd Farnham was fire chief and head of road maintenance, farmer, and general contractor. He was also the island's only policeman. Todd practically ran the island. Their lives and his became intertwined during their adolescence. Sometimes, the boys played pranks on each other and dealt their own justice. Other times, Todd held court with the mischievous boys.

Craig, Bill, Allan, Linc, and Mike, now boys of thirteen and fourteen, had their own twelve-foot Candy boats. Bill said, "Allan told us all year long that his boat wasn't going to leak. For some reason, when our neighbor Oscar Sands helped us put the sailboats into the water, Allan wasn't there. We put Allan's boat out on the mooring, and Craig and I filled it with water." Bill chuckled over the prank now replaying itself in his mind. He said, "Childhood friends managed their own incidents among themselves, but Todd handled those that occurred in the larger community.

"On the west side of the island just north of the stone dock and up on the rise of the hill stood Miss Barney's house.

It was a big old house of twenty to twenty-five rooms. Miss Barney was like something out of the past. She came to the island with her high button boots and long dresses with petticoats under them. One time she fell off the ferry and was kept afloat by those petticoats! Manny Sousa was captain then. He used a boat hook to haul her in," Bill said.

"When Miss Barney left the island at the end of the season, we knew she left a window unlocked on the north side of the house. One night, Mike had a group of the island's young ladies in his black car, the one with the boarded-up window. We were only fourteen, but everyone drove. We got wind of the plan, so Craig, Allan, and I went into the house to wait. As usual the furniture was all draped with sheets. A Bible was in every room. We hid in the closets and when the girls were climbing in the window, we jumped out at them.

"Just then we heard Todd's car coming around the bend. We could tell the sound of his car because it had no muffler. We went one way around the island. Mike went the other. He didn't get caught in the act, but people told Todd that the culprit had an old black car with a wooden window. Mike's was the only one like that. Later, Todd told Mike to find us—which he did. We were guilty by association, just because we were on the island.

"Few people know that the island had a court," Bill continued. "It was held in Todd's kitchen. Millie, Todd's wife, was the judge. She served milk and cookies at the end of the court session. Our sentence was to put a coat of wax on the fire trucks. Those trucks had a lot of wax on them. Todd knew everything that happened here on the island, and only if we didn't straighten out our act would he go to our parents."

The island was a place to play and a place to work. For all of us, the story of our adult lives emerges from the work, the play, and the place. "Craig liked to take things apart," Bill said. "My father brought down a perfect car for the island, but Craig thought the transmission should be taken apart, and he did. Somehow he put the pieces back together, but it shifted sort of backwards. He took the transmission apart again and it worked. He was fourteen. Craig spent hours with his head under the hood of a car."

Around that same time Craig and Bill were hauling gravel for Todd. The gravel had to be moved from the north end of the island to the south end at the Navy base. Bill said, "When we were on the Navy base, Craig got stopped by the shore patrol. They accused him of going too fast and not stopping when he was signaled to do so. The shore patrol chewed him out. Craig said, 'We don't have any brakes.' When the officer asked for his license, of course he didn't have one. He was only fourteen. And, the truck was not registered. The Navy operated by mainland rules." The island functioned by a different set of rules—its own.

"One of Craig's finest cars was a 1935 Buick. It had nothing at all at the front end except for one light mounted on the radiator. No fenders, no grill work, just a light. His favorite car was a 1930 Model A Ford which he used most often as an 'off-road' vehicle.

"Because Craig could fix anything, he was valued as an employee. When he got out of the service, I introduced him to some of my customers on the mainland. We went to ten places and Craig got ten job offers," Bill said.

For about ten years from the early 1960's to the '70's Craig commuted around the island to the west side of the bay—through winter storms and summer fogs—in a tiny Boston Whaler with a 35 horsepower engine. Over the years he worked at other jobs where he was known for his ability to solve problems and fix things. His last job was as head electrician at Hood Enterprises in Portsmouth. And how did Craig commute to work? In a tiny raft, of course.

Craig died in the summer of 1997.

Singly and in pairs, family and neighbors—dressed in shorts and jeans, t-shirts and sweaters—filed down Beach Street in Bristol Colony. Along the way they joined others and talked quietly as they walked under cloudy skies to Bullock's Wharf. Friends formed a half circle, facing the damp breeze and the East Passage of Narragansett Bay— the bay that Craig so loved. Richard Jenness held a Bible. He waited, quietly greeting folks as they arrived, then he began the service in honor of Craig Porter.

The rhythm of the brief service flowed like the sea around us. Richard read from the Bible, "To every thing there is a season, and a time to every purpose under the heaven. A time to be born, and a time to die…," then he gently closed the Bible, held it in his hands and reminisced aloud about his long-time neighbor and friend, Craig Porter. He said, "At four o'clock each day I'd watch for him to come across from Hood in his raft, plywood held up in front of him to keep off the spray." Richard told of his worry that one day Craig might not make it. The raft was flimsy and under powered. He said he became annoyed when Craig ran errands after work and was late, extending that period of concern. Neighbors chuckled. They had memories, too. They knew how singular, how independent Craig had been.

Richard read again, closed his Bible and shared more stories, read and shared. That's how the rhythm went. Then, one by one members of the community stepped forward and faced the gathering to share funny stories that touched our hearts. They told of Craig's love for the island and his generosity of spirit.

That gray morning, family, neighbors and three boyhood friends—Allan, Bill, and Linc—shared fond memories of the living Craig, the Craig whose soul had been formed by the place where he lived.

In memory of Craig L. Porter
1937-1997

Potter's Cove

3 | Black Slacks and a Nor'easter

by Grace Hall McEntee

I don't think very much about what I wear these days, but I've noticed I'm no longer wearing dresses or skirts when I go off island to work as a consultant in schools. Since my slacks wardrobe is rather thin, I recently bought some lined wool crepe slacks, the only slacks they had in black. Yesterday I wore them.

Rain and wind had been in the forecast, but since the ferry is relatively dry I didn't plan to get wet. My umbrella and yellow slicker top would keep me dry for running into this store or that after work.

When I called the ferry at 3:15 to check on the 5:30 run back to the island, the captain said he planned to run the late ferry despite the nor'easter now gearing up for a full-scale blow. Meanwhile, my husband Matt was in Warwick on the other side of the bay, heading home from school in our Sea Hawk.

I arrived early, a quarter to five, at the ferry dock. Part of me knew that my early arrival was to load my purchases and other bags onto the ferry without having to hurry, but another part of me suspected the ferry might not run. The weather had worsened. When the captain saw me, he said, "Grace, we're not running the 5:30. We could hardly get into Homestead during the last run to the island."

The wind whipped up to an April gale and the rain drummed on the cars. Island neighbors, Linda Departhy and Maria Civetti arrived, and we hatched a plan. I'd find a telephone to call Bruce Shaw's Water Taxi. Maria, her daughter Jordana, Linda and I would take the first trip with Bruce from Bristol to the island. Others needing a ride would arrive closer to the scheduled ferry departure and take the next run.

I stood in the rain at the outdoor phone booth with my personal phone book open to Bruce Shaw's number. The telephone would not accept my money, and the numbers blurred on the sodden page. Finally, using a calling card, I made the call to the Water Taxi.

"Hi, Bruce. Are you ready to make a run?" I asked, sure that he would come out, as usual, in the rough seas.

"I'm not sure I can. It's pretty wild out there," he said. "Seas are at least four feet. All the water is trying to rush up the bay and the northeast wind is blowing in the other direction. Call me back in a half hour. I'll go down to check the dock. Maybe the seas will lie down by then." To run the Water Taxi to Bristol, Bruce would have to head right into the storm from his place on the east shore. It is a long run in a nor'easter.

I called Matt, knowing that he had probably just come in from work. "How bad is it out there?" I asked. He'd tell me if he thought it was too risky to come to Bristol to pick me up. Running the boat from our house meant cutting across the waves or at least catching them on the port bow. It wasn't like heading right into them.

"No problem," he said. "The lines in Blount's Dock are a pain. It's high tide and tough to get through them, but I'll come get you."

By the time I returned to the ferry parking lot, my nephew Michael had arrived, along with some other commuters. Michael decided to go with Matt and me. Chris Dunbar chose to stay on the mainland with a friend. The rest waited to make the second call to Bruce.

Matt arrived. Again, he said, "It's not that bad." By this time I had traded my wool jacket for a slicker and had put on my rain boots, but I did not have the bottom slickers to keep my legs dry. Ah, well, I thought, the pants will dry.

Michael and I stepped onto the boat and put on life preservers. Matt turned to me and said, "Would you hold down the top on our dry box? The cover blew open and broke the hinges on my way home from school." Ours is an open boat. Sitting as far back in the stern as possible, the dry box is two feet tall and four feet wide. In lieu of a cabin, it has served us well to protect groceries, school bags, and books from heavy seas and driving rain.

My left hand gripped a line secured to the portside cleat, and my right hand held the top of the box. It was an awkward position, but the ride from Bristol to Blount's is a short one, four miles at most. Michael stood in the lee of the center console and windshield. When we were still inside the harbor, I said, "Hey, this isn't bad at all."

Then the boat roared out of Bristol Harbor and beyond the protection of the land. We slid through troughs of waves, cresting four to six feet. The boat rocked and lurched, with the wind now on our starboard stern quarter. With my hand on the box in the stern, I was a sitting duck. Each wave curled, broke, and drenched my face and body with its spray. Michael's khakis turned from light tan to darker tan as the rain washed down his slicker and absorbed into the cotton. Matt drove with his full slicker on. He had already been drenched on his ride home from school and changed into dry clothes. He meant to keep them dry, too.

"Wow, look at that," Michael said, as we pulled into the docking area at Blount's. Ordinarily above the high water mark, the northwest side of the dock sat under a foot of water. Of course, on that side the docking cleats were also under water. Matt swung the boat around. Michael and I leaned forward and tried to catch a cross tie line hanging directly in our path, two to three feet above the water. It was in place for another boat. We missed it and the tip of our bow caught on the line that we intended to go under.

Waves and currents drove us toward the west side of the iron, boat-eating monster of a dock. "Grab the line!" said Matt, knowing that if we hit the iron siding our engine would be chewed to bits. "Pull the boat!" he said. The three of us grabbed the cross tie line that had caused the problem. With all our strength we pulled on the line and drew the boat toward the east side of the dock and out of immediate danger.

The boat bobbed inside the washtub of a docking area in the chaos of the storm. I stepped ever so carefully onto the bow, bobbed up and down with the rhythm of the waves, and stepped onto the dock with a line in my hand. Matt hung onto the cross tie line that had caused our original problem. Michael tossed a second line to me, but a wave crashed onto the dock and washed the line into the water before I could grab it. I secured our bow line onto the cleat on the dock. Michael's next throw worked, and I cleated the second line. Each wave crashed over the dock sending spray high into the air, and the sea washed over the dock.

The dock at Blount's is a concrete apron with drain holes. Despite the holes, water was six inches deep on the dock near the stern of the boat. I sloshed through the water, which felt warm on my feet and ankles, compared to the cold black pants now plastered to my legs.

Michael stepped onto the dock while Matt tossed a line to the other side for a cross tie. I went to get it, where the water now was more than a foot deep. Mat yelled, "I'll get it," so Michael and I piled into the truck. I was cold, and it felt good to squish against Michael.

But when Matt came around to look for the line he had thrown, he could not find it. The waves had sucked it back into deeper water. Michael and I got out of the truck and went back to help Matt finish securing the Sea Hawk for the night. We pulled the boat in so that Matt could re-board. Michael held the boat while Matt tossed our cross tie line to the other side for the second time. I sloshed into water up to my knees to retrieve the line and Matt came around to secure it.

We drove Michael to Homestead Dock to pick up his truck, and we came back to our own warm house. Matt had started a fire and hung his first set of wet clothes before he had come to get me. I called Linda to ask whether the rest of the group had gotten home with the Water Taxi. Mark answered and said he had served her dinner and she was now relaxing with a cigarette. I knew how glad she was to be home.

When I hung up the phone, I glanced down at my black slacks—dry clean only. The knees bulged out and they looked as though they had been filled with lumpy mashed potatoes.

In a hot bath I soaked until my body was deeply warmed, and then Matt soaked. We ate leftover turkey casserole for dinner. That night we slept like babies.

Days like this are great for stretching muscles and

releasing tension when nothing else matters except the wind and the rain. What may seem like a terrible inconvenience to landlubbers is really the stuff of our island adventures. But days like this one do make it difficult to maintain a professional wardrobe, particularly one that includes black slacks, *dry clean only.*

4 | Remembering Benny

by Grace Hall McEntee

"So many people from around the country vis-
ited the Braytons, and they all called Benny 'Pa,' but I could
never call him Pa," my husband Matt said. "I called him
Benny. He was like a father figure, but he was a good buddy,
too. He always welcomed me with a big hug. 'Hi Matt,'
he'd say, and he'd give me the hug."

Matt and I met Benny, his wife Idene, and the rest of
the Braytons in 1980 shortly after we moved to Prudence
Island. Benny was seventy-one at the time, and we
remained good friends for the twelve years until Benny died
in the spring of 1992. During those years, Benny and Idene
spent their summers in their little white house at the north
end, close to the rocky beach. They were our neighbors on
Prudence Island.

One morning not too long ago, Matt and I sat at our kitchen table remembering Benny. For the most part I listened to Matt talk about his old friend. "I used to like to see him in his farmer jeans with no shirt on," Matt said. "He was a little guy, brown and weathered year round, and he didn't mind getting dirty." For Matt, getting dirty is a positive quality. For him, it means diving into work, body and soul.

Benny often drove over to our house in his pickup truck. He'd slide down out of the truck, then go around to open the passenger door. Heidi, his huge black Lab, ever so gently leaped down from the seat. Matt and I always walked out to greet Benny. When he saw us, he smiled and chuckled and looked right at us with sparkling eyes.

I didn't remember how Matt and Benny's friendship started, so I asked Matt about it. "I met him and that was it," Matt said. "I used to see him down the way and I'd wave to him. He'd wave back at me. Like a boater or quahogger. Then for some reason he cared about me. Like your father, he liked me.

"Later, he needed somebody to help him and I wanted to help," Matt said. "He seemed overburdened, always working on that place. It didn't matter whether it was to fix it for himself or his family or to fix it up to sell. It was the old Prudence Island way, always fixing things up. Getting the house to look good was important to him."

Benny's sons had built him a new home on the mainland, a beautiful house that had plenty of room for

Benny and Idene and for any of their friends, children, or grandchildren who chose to visit. But here on the island Benny felt driven to fix up their little place.

"We worked to put his kitchen together," Matt said. "We got all the wood at the dump. He loved taking stuff from the dump. Just like me. He'd say, 'Look what I found at the dump today,' and he'd be happy.

"He was a good guy to be around. One of the nice things for me was that he knew I would do anything for him. The night before he died I talked about getting a lower unit for a boat engine for his son Roger.

"He didn't mind asking me for help. He'd say, 'I noticed what a nice job you did on my doorway.' That was his way of saying thank you.

"He'd help me, too. He was a pretty good mechanic. Learned it by himself, I think. He'd raise the idle or fix the carburetor or the brakes. He loved jumping into his own truck to get it running better.

"I picked up the blue truck so Benny and I could use some parts. That was the deal. We'd keep it in his yard and we could both share it. He got under the truck and took out the gas tank, no problem. " As Matt talked, I couldn't help thinking that they were like two teenagers, the way they'd share what they had without thinking about who owned what.

"Benny wanted to get his boat running just right," Matt continued. "In his later years he thought he'd get back out on the boat and do some quahogging. But he never did. It annoyed Benny that he had so much trouble getting the boat out of the water and onto the trailer in Bristol. He couldn't back the truck up and see what he was doing. He used to tell me stuff like that.

"He couldn't hear for anything, either. He said that he had a ringing in one ear, and it bothered him so much that he had it taken care of. After that he heard no sound in that ear at all."

Benny did love that boat. It was a treat to see Benny and Idene sitting on the bench seat, side by side, as they zoomed away from the Prudence shore. Despite the problem he had trailering his boat, he still launched it each time they commuted to the island—until the summer he died. They were in their eighties by then.

"Benny wasn't a quitter," Matt said with admiration. His sons might say that Benny worried too much over projects, especially over the Prudence house. Matt identified with Benny's stick-to-itiveness. It was a quality they had in common. "He stuck to whatever he needed to fix, but there was so much to fix. That's why his garage was always so cluttered. Like mine," he said. "Before we had a garage, he let me use his. That was a nice thing.

"When he was coming to the island, I'd bail out Benny's rowboat. It sat out on his mooring most of the time. He appreciated that. He'd say, 'Thanks, Matt.'" Benny was a man of few words. He said only what needed to be said.

While Matt spoke about Benny and his rowboat, I remembered one October night before a storm. Benny called to ask Matt to pull his dinghy up from the beach. We were both teaching on the mainland in Warwick at the time, and our chores were often done in the darkness of early evening. As I took the clothes down from the line, Matt went off to pull up Benny's dinghy. I hadn't even finished taking down the clothes when I heard Matt's truck tires crunching along the gravel road to our house. I turned to see the truck lights swing like searchlights around the corner and knew something was wrong. He jumped out of the truck and said, "I need your help." I grabbed my sweater and went with him.

We pulled up to Benny's garage. Matt slid from his seat in the truck and hurried around to the waterfront side. I hustled along behind him. As if mute, he stopped and pointed. Above the garage were two bedrooms for family and guests to stay when they came to visit. Sliding glass doors opened onto a deck, which stretched over the entrance to the garage, facing the water.

I gasped in horror. The deck draped down as though it were made of fabric, one corner nearly touching the ground.

In his attempt to pull the heavy dinghy up from the beach, around the corner, and into the back yard, Matt had used one deck support as a fulcrum. He attached a rope to the dinghy, looped it around the support, and tied it to the bumper of his truck. Using that method, Matt thought the heavy boat could be pulled to the spot where Benny wanted it. Standing there beside him, I experienced the horror that Matt must have felt as he drove the truck forward and saw the deck collapse behind him as the supports gave out.

For the next couple of hours, Matt jacked up the deck as I jockeyed new supports under it. Benny was coming to the island the following weekend. Matt wanted to fix the deck so that Benny would not have something else to worry about. Every afternoon after school that week, Matt was over at Benny's repairing and strengthening the deck. "It's better now than it ever was," Matt said one day. And I knew he felt that it was ready for Benny.

Benny Brayton was born in East Greenwich, Rhode Island, in January of 1909. His mother brought him to the north end of Prudence Island when he was one year old. "The doctor said I wouldn't live. I had pneumonia and some other things. Well, I lived," he said one day as I listened to Benny remembering.

When he was five years old his family moved to the Grace house—also known as the Garland Estate—at the north end of the island where his parents were caretakers. "When my father was forty years old," Benny said, "something popped in his head. It was an aneurysm, I think. I was eight years old then. He lived in an institution until he was eighty. I hardly remember him.

"I used to stop at Johnny Gomes.' He was the oysterman who lived with his wife in the Oysterman's shack, that's Prew's house, a couple of houses down from you, Grace," he said. "Johnny was a little man. His wife weighed four times what he did. They had a pony and a cart and they would go down to meet the ferry. I used to stop at their house on the way to school and she would give me coffee. It was a good life here. I had a horse, a dog, and a gun. What more could a boy want? I rode my horse to school. I let it loose and it would hang around until school was over.

"At school I hated Eleanor Chase," he said. "She'd run and tell the teacher on us. We took her down in the woods one day. We were going to hang her, but of course, we didn't. Her sister Barbara was more of a tomboy."

Benny's sister-in-law Emily Brayton became the teacher. "I liked her," he said, "but I didn't like to go to school. I wasn't a good student. When I fell in love, around eighth grade, I could only sit there and stare at my love. She sat near the window. Finally, Miss Brayton moved me next to her, and I think that cured me.

"Miss Brayton cramped my style, though. She boarded with us at the north end of the island. When she moved in, I had to abandon my horse commute and take the carriage. I didn't like her then," he said, remembering his boyish rebellion. Benny went to the Prudence Island School until he was fourteen.

"What about the school at the north end?" I asked. "Oh, that was before my time," Ben said. "My mother and her sister went to that school years ago. At the time they lived on Patience Island [a small island west of Prudence] and they rowed across the gap every day to go to school."

"Even in the wintertime?" I said. He nodded. I gasped in amazement. The distance is short, but a strong current flows between the islands. In a storm or in the ice, rowing across the gap would be a mighty challenge.

Benny said that his grandmother lived way up at the north end where only house foundations exist today. That area was all farmland when he was a child, even up to the time when Benny and Idene were first married. "The cedars are new in the last forty years," he said.

Benny brought Idene to visit Prudence Island for the first time when she was seventeen, the year before she and Benny married. The following year, they moved to the island, where they spent the first fourteen years of their marriage. They raised their family—five boys and a girl—at the Grace house, where they were caretakers, just as Benny's parents had been caretakers before them.

Idene had grown up in Barrington where her family raised dairy cows, "Holsteins for quantity and Guernseys for cream," she had said one day when we sat with them, talking about their early days together. During that same conversation Benny had said, "I wasn't ever going to get married." He turned to Idene, his wife of sixty years, as he spoke. It was a look of love. "My brother hadn't done so well," he said. "I wasn't interested. Then I met Idene. I took her out to dinner and, boy, did she eat! Then I knew if she was going to eat like that, she'd probably cook. My brother's wife didn't cook."

Benny's father had been a fisherman, and in later years Benny and his sons became fishermen—some of his boys still are. But Benny talked about raising hay up at the north end of the island, too. He used a threshing machine to get the seed. "One year I sold the seed and made a hundred dollars, an enormous amount in those days," he said. "With the money I bought myself a new suit, dark blue, with a tie, a white scarf, and a bowler hat. That's how I dressed in those days.

"My father had an old boat called the *Anna M*," Benny said. "He sailed the boat up from Florida to be converted to a dragger for fishing. After my father was gone, the boat sat on the beach going to pot. Captain Herzog was running the *Harvest*, a summer ferry, owned by Halsey Chase. It went to and from Prudence, but during the winter he abandoned us and went to Florida. Then we were stuck without transportation. The first Prudence Navigation Company was formed to provide the island with year-round ferry service and the *Anna M* was converted into a ferry for that purpose. The cabin was changed and, of course, an engine installed."

As Matt and I finished our breakfast and wrapped up our conversation about Benny and Idene, he remembered that every morning Idene made bacon and eggs for Benny. She was making breakfast when he died, just like any other morning.

As Matt and I cleared the table, we tried to imagine how Idene felt when she found Benny on the morning that he died. Idene told us that Benny had gotten up and put on his shirt, a gift from his daughter. He joked with her about how much mileage he had gotten out of that shirt, and then went outside to work on his car. She said that it bothered Benny that he couldn't get the Oldsmobile going. "He worried about stuff like that," Matt reminded me. "He wouldn't sleep well because of it." When Benny didn't come in for breakfast, she called him and then went out to look for him. Idene found Benny beside the car.

Matt and I thought that, given his choice, Benny might have wanted to die working on his car while he waited for Idene to make his breakfast. If we had our choice, we would have wanted our friend to live forever.

Over time Matt and I have learned to savor friends—like Benny—who are a generation older than we are. They are loving and wise. Part of their wisdom is that they know how to make others, like us, feel useful. They teach us how to give of ourselves, and, in helping them, we learn a little bit about renovating houses or fixing cars and a lot about living our lives.

5 | The Critter

by Grace Hall McEntee

The water was choppy on that morning in late April, 1997. Exceptionally high tides had not been predicted, nor had the night time seas raged in a springtime storm. But the pre-dawn high tide had risen above Blount's Dock. The sea had washed beyond its ordinary bounds to thrust a denizen from its watery habitat. There stranded on the dock helplessly waving its arms and legs, lay a strange little critter.

I picked it up and cradled it in the palm of my hand. The pale pink almost translucent body extended beyond my fingertips at one end and beyond the heel of my hand on the other. Its segmented body looked very much like a lobster's tail. "What does a baby lobster look like?" I asked myself. As soon as I asked the question, I knew for sure that what I had in my hand was not a baby lobster.

The tail end narrowed to flatness, like a lobster's tail, but it was the head that made me feel that I held a gentle ET, a harmless creature from an alien world. Four antennae, two or three inches long, sprang straight from what appeared to be its neck. Between the two pairs of antennae sat two tiny bright blue eyes that made me smile. They looked like beads on a child's toy, wildly colorful and opaque. Would such a creature show expression? I could read none, yet I knew that it was looking at me as I held it in my palm, its arms and legs groping ineffectually at the air.

I'm not sure why this critter touched my heart. By some standards it might have been judged ugly, perhaps untouchable. It could have been precisely that which caused me to search for beauty in its tiny eyes. Or maybe the beauty was there all along and my task was to discover it.

By now, the surface of the water had dropped to several feet below the level of the still wet dock. Carefully cupping the critter in my hands, I knelt down, leaned toward the water, and ever so gently let it go. Like a leaf detaching itself from a tree in a light wind, the critter left my hands and drifted, until it reached the sandy bottom, where it lay on its back. "Oh, it's dead," I thought. But slowly, with the help of a light current, the critter turned over and crept away.

That night I called my daughter, a biologist and, like

me, a teacher. Proud that I had observed the critter so that I could describe it, I told her about its pink body and many legs.

"How many legs did it have?" she asked.

I smiled sheepishly to myself. "A lotta," I said.

She laughed with me. "Could it have been ten?"

"Maybe." Why didn't I count them? I had meant to examine it so very carefully. I even had a camera in my bag and might have caught the image so that someone more skillful than I would have the privilege of identifying the critter. I provided other details of its appearance and she promised to research it.

During the week a friend and former harbormaster came to the house. I described the critter and asked what it might be. He had seen fishermen bring them up in their nets. He thought it was called a "manta" shrimp, not that uncommon, but more common in the South where waters are warmer.

Eventually, I spoke with a fisherman, one whose daily business it is to identify what is in the net that he brings up from the bottom. "Oh, that's a mantis shrimp. You know, like a praying mantis. They are fierce predators. Did you notice the front legs? They reach out and nab their prey."

A few days later as I kicked a stone along a smooth part of the road, I thought again about the little critter. "Hey," I said to myself, "even fierce predators can be beautiful. Like owls and fox and—humans."

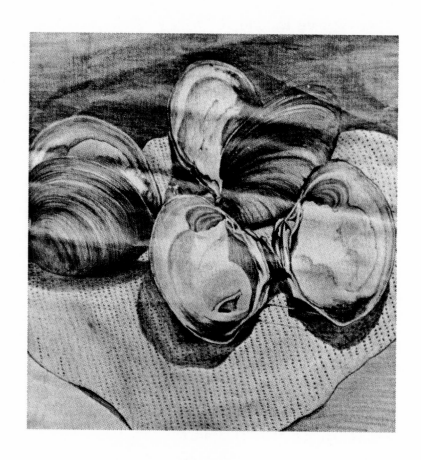

Quahog

6 | The Rogue Wave

By Grace Hall McEntee

Weather sparks my interest. Like John Ghiorse, a meteorologist and professional weather forecaster, I talk about the weather. With a twinkle in his eye, Matt calls me "John" for short. Once, however, an unpredictable weather event occurred that I tucked away and did not share. It seemed more like fiction than fact, and I didn't want to be known as a teller of false tales.

Recently, I read a liberating book, at least for a storm buff like me. In *The Perfect Storm* Sebastian Junger writes about a series of storms that occurred in October, 1991, storms which came together to form "the perfect storm" off the Grand Banks. The story recounts what may have happened to the fishermen caught in the storm. While that "perfect storm" exceeded many times what we would ever

encounter in Narragansett Bay, some of what Junger said
in the story, particularly about rogue waves, felt validating:

> Scientists understand how waves work, but not
> exactly how *huge* ones work. There are rogue waves
> out there, in other words, that seem to exceed the
> forces generating them.

I was thrilled to read this. "Yes, yes," I said, " . . . exceed
the forces generating them . . . ." I had experienced a *huge*
wave, at least for Narragansett Bay and for our small
twenty-one foot Sea Ox. Later in the book, Junger goes on
to say, "In the dry terminology of naval architecture, these
are called 'non-negotiable waves.' Mariners call them 'freak
seas' or 'rogue waves.'"

When we first moved to Prudence Island in 1980, Luther
Blount warned us about squalls that spontaneously erupt
on Narragansett Bay. "They can capsize a fifty-foot boat,"
he said. I think he mentioned rogue waves, too. So, when
we began our daily commute to the west side of the bay,
we knew rogue waves existed. Like most, who travel
regularly by water, we decided to take the calculated risk.
Rogue waves are rare.

In the twenty years since then we have experienced
feisty squalls and other kinds of storms conjured up by the
bay and the sky. In all that time, however, we have
experienced only one rogue wave. I had forgotten that rogue
waves exist until one mid-December morning in 1991.

That morning sparkled with a clear intensity that makes
winter mornings special on the water. The northwest wind

blew briskly at eighteen to twenty miles per hour and the temperature was a comfortable thirty-one degrees. During the twilight between darkness and daybreak, Matt and I loaded the Sea Ox with our gear for the day—bags containing school clothes, my briefcase bursting with student compositions. We set off in a northerly direction toward Providence Point, the first leg of our commute to Warwick.

In the morning I am the pilot of the boat. It is my best time of day. I am fresh and alert, and I love to drive. Matt, who takes longer to wake up, sat facing the stern and drank his morning coffee. Except for the sound of the engine, it was a quiet time—not because an unwritten law of the sea abides, but because we were at peace.

Sometimes I thought about school as I traveled, but usually I tuned in to the world around me. Still below the horizon, the sun worked its kaleidoscope. Burnished pewter and coke-bottle green shimmered along the water's surface.

We skimmed along the tops of the waves. Traveling into a moderate breeze is exciting because a tension exists between what is possible and what might be foolhardy. The pilot of the boat must anticipate a change in the pattern of the waves or in the intensity of the wind. As soon as that change occurs, to avoid a jolt she must pull back the throttle and take each wave deliberately, one at a time.

The waves appeared uniform in size and shape. As colors shifted and slithered around me, I kept the throttle steady.

In any series of waves, a larger wave exists. Some say it

is the mythical ninth wave. In *Papillon*, a nonfiction novel, the prisoner escapes from shore on a raft. He waits for the ninth wave, pushes his raft into the water, using the suction from the huge wave to pull it out beyond the breakers. In Tennyson's *Idylls of the King*, the infant King Arthur arrives in fire on the ninth wave.

As I skimmed along on what seemed at first to be a washboard of evenly spaced waves of uniform height, I watched for that larger wave in the series. Whether or not it is the ninth one, it is always there.

I saw a white line in the distance, what seemed to be a wave, larger than the rest. I was in the vicinity of Bear Point where the waves increase in height from trough to crest, so I pulled back on the throttle and abandoned the skimming. Each wave now appeared unique—this one a green curler, the next a shiny, gray humpback. The wind was blowing directly from the north. I took one or two waves at ten o'clock off the port bow, then I switched to take another at two o'clock off the starboard bow, tacking back and forth so that we could run in a relatively straight course, due north. All the time I watched the wave ahead, the one that was larger than the rest, its white frothy crest a clear line now in the near distance.

On the hook just inside our three-sided open cabin and not a foot from my left hand on the steering wheel, hung my life preserver. During stormy weather or in high seas I always wear it, but ordinarily there is no need to wear it on a morning like this. I felt safe. My feet were planted wide apart on the floor, forming a triangle to keep me steady, knees slightly flexed to cushion the jounce from each wave. The compass heading was due north; the tachometer read 3800 rpms. And the wave was just ahead.

What had been rather routine up to this point changed in an instant.

Suddenly the wave I was watching became the only wave on the bay. A wall of water—vertically lined, opaque, greenish white—rose from the sea. The center of the wave was at eye level. Its crest curled above me. It appeared that our bow would cut through the lower third of the wave.

How will I take this wave? Off the port bow? Off the starboard? How big can it possibly be, ten feet, twelve? I forgot that Matt was in the boat or that I should alert him. No fear muddied my mind. My focus was on the wave and the boat. I rejected taking the wave on the starboard bow or the port bow. The boat would flip like a balsa toy. We'd take this one straight on. If the bow cut the wave, we'd be swamped, but at least we'd have the chance of remaining upright as the water ran out the bailing holes in the stern.

The boat rose higher, higher, and higher. I held the wheel tightly knowing I was no longer in control. We seemed poised out in space. Then, BOOM! We slammed down into the next trough—beyond the rogue wave.

"What the hell was that?" yelled Matt, who had been dwelling in his own morning world as he finished his coffee. "I flew right out of my seat," he said.

I burst out laughing, giddy from relief, but appalled at

the sudden realization that I had forgotten to tell him all that had been happening. "Oh, Matt, I'm sorry you missed it. That wasn't any regular old ninth wave, that was a rogue wave."

"How do you know?" he asked.

"When you see it, you know. It was different from any other wave we've seen," I said. And a gap of experience yawned between us. I shivered as I noticed my life preserver still on its hook.

7 | First Summer

by Josie Avery

Family friends, the Harringtons, introduced the Avery clan to the island in the summer of 1963. We stayed with Mrs. Harrington's parents, Grandpa and Grandma Hudson. Grandpa Hudson, although reticent in the fashion of many Yankees, welcomed us to their home. The house has changed greatly in the intervening years, but I remember it as a gray shingled Queen Ann cape, filled with antiques and camp-like features. The cottage was in a perfect setting—across the street from the beach and a few minutes walk to the counter of penny candy at Marcy's.

On summer mornings my friend Sara and I charged out the door with bathing suits on and the prerequisite old sneakers to protect our feet from the rocky beach. We spent hours in the water, holding contests to see how long we could hold our breath, how far we could walk before the water was over our heads—doing the things kids do. When we weren't in the water, we explored the beach as we walked down to the lighthouse or sometimes grabbed pails from the house to pick blueberries.

Tired from our morning of fun, Sara and I headed back to the cottage porch. In the afternoons we lazed around on the porch swing and flipped through *Good Housekeeping* magazines, *Readers' Digest*, and old comic books. Sometimes, we would nag our parents for pennies, nickels, and dimes to buy candy at Marcy's. But most times we were just content lying against the deep cushions of that porch swing.

When Sara and I saw Grandpa Hudson walk down to the beach with his quahogging gear, we tried to guess what would be for dinner—stuffies, red chowder, how 'bout both? Outfitted with an inner tube and a metal basket tied to his belt loop, he walked slowly back and forth in the water, raking the rocky bottom, and stopped only when he was sure he had enough. With his basket full of quahogs Grandpa Hudson walked to the kitchen and poured the bounty into the sink. Grandma Hudson set to work on his catch of the day. The smell of her cooking wafted through the house and reached our haven on the porch.

Called for dinner, a big gang of people—eleven in all— squeezed around the dining room table to eat Grandpa's delicious catch of the day. When the table was cleared after dinner and before going to bed, the kids played a card game called "pitch" with the grownups.

Occasionally our bedtime hour was extended when someone shouted—"Let's go for a ride!" Mrs. Harrington sat behind the wheel of Grandpa Hudson's car, my mother beside her—both smoking and laughing—while the kids piled into the backseat. Cars on Prudence at that time were ancient, and so we always had the impression we were living inside an old movie. Grandpa's car was a 1950 silver Pontiac the kids called "The Silver Streak." I remember the cloth seats that felt prickly and weird on the backs of my legs whenever I wore shorts.

One such ride took us to the north part of the island, up the Neck toward the former Garland Estate, which we kids thought of as "the castle," since the old stone house had a very Gothic look. It wasn't the first time we had driven there, but this time just before we reached Potter's Cove we started to spin a story. I must have started the story because it starred a horse and every story I spun at nine had a horse in it. The story went something like this:

Once upon a time there was a beautiful girl who lived in the castle. She owned a beautiful white stallion that she loved very much. He was very skittish and wild. One night in the middle of a terrible thunderstorm, she heard the horse kicking the walls of his stall and screaming out in fear. She knew she must comfort him. So she put on her robe and hurried out the side door to the stable. When she got to the stable, the white stallion was still screaming and kicking, his nostrils flared in fear. The young girl was afraid he might hurt himself and break his legs. So she decided to go into his stall and calm him down. When she opened the gate, the stallion saw his opportunity and bolted out the stall door. The young girl grabbed the rope of his halter trying to stop him. In a moment of sheer will, she vaulted onto his back and they flew out the stable door. All around them the sky flashed, and the wind and rain whipped them forward. The young girl made every effort to control the horse, but she did not have the strength. As they continued down the road away from the castle, she lost her hold and fell into the pond near Potter's Cove. She groped upwards hoping her steed would return to her rescue, but he did not and she drowned. And so some nights when it's particularly stormy or the moon is full and you look at the pond, you may see her slender arm rise up grasping for her stallion's rope lead.

The End.

This was the daily rhythm of my first summer on the island. Sara and I swam, explored the island's rocky beaches and its lighthouse, spun stories and shared our dreams on the porch swing—as only nine-year-old girls can.

8 | Gathering Stories, Recording History

by Grace Hall McEntee

Some islanders remember when war touched Prudence Island. Because it sits in the middle of Narragansett Bay—the corridor for traffic from the Atlantic Ocean to the capitol city Providence—the island assumed a strategic role during World War II. The Army established a Searchlight Unit on Prudence Island as part of the Narragansett Bay Defense Training.

During the summer of 1942 troops landed at Sand Point on the east side of Prudence Island. They set up camp mid island, along what is now known as the old Army Road.

Forty years later, Ros Bosworth, then editor of the *Sakonnet Times* and the *Bristol Phoenix*, invited me to write a story about the Searchlight Unit. Ros remembered hearing soldiers' singing, but could not remember the song. He told me that Marcy had married one of the soldiers, Danny Shea. Ros, himself, was too young for the Army at the time, but the installation did make an impression on him. "There is still a well there that the Army drilled," he said, "and I think the man in charge was Sergeant Truax."

With these details and the names of a few islanders who might talk with me about the Searchlight Unit, I rode off on my bicycle to gather information from islanders who had witnessed this historical event.

I began with Manny Sousa. Manny was a small, wiry man with a face etched by his life-long relationship with the sea. He sat with his wife in their cozy home south of Sand Point. I faced Manny. Beyond him lay the bay's East Passage, where he had served as engineer and captain of the *Prudence I*, an island ferry. He focused on the sea. And I listened.

"Yes," he said, "the soldiers in the Searchlight Unit came to the island on Army boats. I was working as the engineer on the *Prudence I* at the time, so I hardly saw them. Later, the Navy came to the island. Their workers traveled by ferry."

According to Manny, a Searchlight Unit was needed because Germans were coming up the bay. A submarine net was stretched from Newport to Castle Hill, but it was still possible for a sub to sneak under when the net was opened to allow other ships through. "The water around that area may be a hundred feet deep," he said. "A German sub sank off Block Island. Salvage people wanted to get it, but the German government said no because it is a grave.

"There were spies everywhere," Manny said. "One time there was a stranger on the island. He was taking pictures every day. He would not talk to anyone, but he took pictures in Bristol of the Herreshoff operation, too. They were building minesweepers and torpedo boats. He took pictures of the Melville fuel depot across the East Passage and of Quonset, west of the island. Eventually, somebody called the F.B.I. They sent people over to watch him, and they picked him up as a spy."

From the Sousa household I rode to the Bacons' at Sunset Hill Farm, where the Prudence Island Vineyard was still in operation. Natalie Chase Bacon moved about her dark kitchen in the farmhouse at the top of Sunset Hill. She was a large woman, with an aristocratic manner and a country smile. Natalie remembered the Searchlight Unit. Where Manny's focus was on the sea, hers was on the land.

The Searchlight Unit was practically in the Bacons' present front yard. "The Army leased the land," she said. "They removed the Paul Chase house that had been used as a boarding house and built a barracks there. Later on, Milton Chase used the lumber from the boarding house to construct the Prudence Inn."

She said, "The Army trucks really did not fit into the pastoral scene of the hill. Cows grazed over the four hundred acres surrounding that area. When the Army fenced the area off, the cows were moved and the Army stayed. It was too bad that they had to cut the beautiful trees, but the Army's presence didn't cause any fear in people. Really, it was a feeling that maybe they would save lives." According to Natalie, the Army came to the island because of the fear of German attack.

"They did come to visit sometimes, too," Natalie said. "Nate rode around with the Army men, sometimes to the Navy base to the movies."

Natalie and Bill's son Nate remembered the soldiers on the old Army Road, too. He said, "I was the mascot, only three or four years old at the time. I would ride on the truck with the soldiers. I guess they were there for strategic purposes, to guard the bay."

Where the Army Road intersects with Broadway and down a bit to the west lived Todd and Millie Farnham. Before my bike riding days and my gathering details for the story on the Searchlight Unit, Todd had been teaching me how to play guitar. For years Todd and Millie had been performers on radio. She played the steel guitar, and he plucked the banjo or strummed an acoustic guitar. They played Bluegrass songs and sang in harmony. After our playing one night, I asked if he would talk with me about the Searchlight Unit.

Todd sat in his chair in the tiny living room, facing south. His white bushy eyebrows served as expressive antennae for his sparkling eyes, and he spoke with a bit of a twang, that suggested origins southwest of New England. "Well, for most of the time when the Searchlight Unit was here I was off on business myself in England. But I did go up to the barracks now and then for a cup of coffee with the men. The first time, I was given a cup and told to dip it into the tin. The coffee barrel looked like a garbage can. I plunged my cup in for the brew and hit bottom.

The can was filled almost all the way to the top with grounds. There was a little coffee floating on top." He chuckled and went on.

"Up there they had a generator, a searchlight, and a barracks, much like the barracks that were constructed elsewhere up and down the bay. The barracks used gas stoves in their Army field kitchen, but they heated with soft coal and left some there when they pulled out. They borrowed town equipment, the grader, to fix their road—the Army Road. They towed the grader with a GMC 6x6." Todd would know about town equipment and its use. For some years, Todd had been in charge of island road maintenance.

"Anyway, there was a spotlight mounted on the ground to search out the planes overhead. It seems to me [it was more about] propaganda than anything else. There was a necessity of keeping the war consciousness going. We could have no bonfires on the beach. On Fourth of July we built a bonfire, but we were called and told to put it out. Millie and I were working on the radio at the time. When someone called in a request for a song, we could sing a song, but not the one requested because of the danger of coded messages."

Eventually, I made my way over to one of the other Chase houses along the backbone of the island. There, Arlene Cramm Butler talked eagerly over several sessions. I had already met Arlene in her garden and knew her to have a fine mind for detail. At a large bare rectangular table in a spacious room just off her kitchen, she talked about what she remembered with apparent clarity.

"The Searchlight Unit was a loose group under the Army Corps of Engineers at Fort Adams in Newport, from the 277th Regimental Anti-aircraft Battalion. They were here from June 1942 to just after the war. The government was making war preparations for the European front in England. The men in the Searchlight Unit were draftees from all over the country, from the hills of Virginia to Connecticut. There were only six to eight at a time. They would serve for a period of months then they would be replaced by others. Really, they were a stop-gap group, until the Navy could prepare their forces to take over the task of air surveillance.

"Milton and Sara Chase owned the Prudence Inn at the time. There was a jukebox and dancing. Often people would just sit around and play cards and talk. It was a comfortable nightspot for the soldiers and for the young people on the island.

"The Searchlight Unit had a sergeant-in-charge, a driver, one or two radiomen, a cook and housekeeper, who would get his supplies by a supply boat from Fort Adams. The last sergeant-in-charge there was Danny Shea, who became Marcy's first husband. One soldier served on patrol and a couple of extras replaced these men when they were on leave. They had a barracks, a gun placement, radio shack, and a well, which was closed up when they left.

"Although the beaches along the ocean front were guarded by the Navy, there were not enough personnel to guard the beaches of Prudence in Narragansett Bay. Houses here were used for signaling. Positioning of the shades was one signaling method.

"A couple of times the men at the searchlight battalion were attacked, the searchlight was broken, and the attackers were never caught.

"Why was the searchlight battalion established here?" she said. "They were needed for radio contact, to search for enemy planes, and as a possible cover for other operations. The Nazi strength was known and the possibility of Nazi attack seemed real.

"The big defense system was in Bristol. Up on the hill of Bristol there was a signal light and there was, of course, the one on Prudence. For lack of better equipment, they would communicate via these light signals and also by radio signals."

Arlene flicked back in memory. "We really should have known that the war was coming. We had an international group of guests staying at the house. They told us that during the 1930's old tramp steamers were dismantled in junkyards and taken to Japan. At the outbreak of the war we were under manned and under supplied. The Navy, for example, could not handle the job on Prudence Island. The Army provided the Searchlight Unit until the Navy moved in at the south end. Then the Army was transferred to other areas. They served as guards at Fort Wetherill on the island of Jamestown in Narragansett Bay, which was closed as an Army operation and used as a reeducation center for prisoners, as was Fort Devens. Then they went off to Europe." Arlene finished her story and I my visit with her.

Later, I wrote to the General Services Administration, National Archives and Records Service, in Washington, DC, to corroborate information about the Army Searchlight Unit on Prudence Island. Assistant Chief Edwin R. Coffee from the National Archives responded to my inquiry about the World War II Searchlight Unit on Prudence Island:

> A further examination of our harbor defense records of Narragansett Bay failed to reveal any units stationed there [on Prudence Island].

Ros Bosworth's "special edition" never happened and my notes sat in a folder for sixteen years. But, somehow that didn't really matter because the "assignment" led me to something that continues today—an interest in my neighbors and the wealth of experience that each carries. I feel thankful to have written the stories they told me—since no "official" record exists. I also thank each one for teaching me a bit about what my mother said I needed to learn when I was a little girl—how to listen.

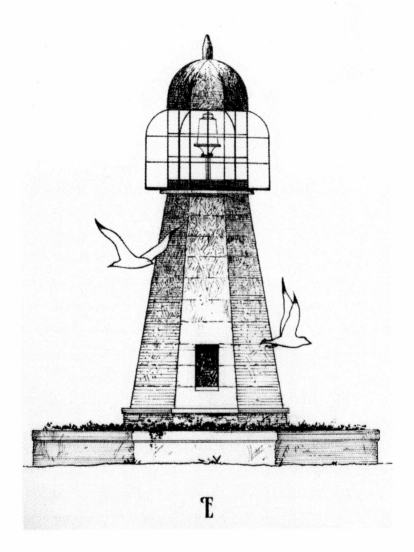

Sand Point Lighthouse

9 | Mystery on PI
1996 – 2000

by Grace Hall McEntee

The count was down. Everybody was talking about it.

During the 1996 bow hunting season hunters had taken over two hundred deer. At that time the herd seemed big enough to recover. Even after the season ended, deer fed in the usual places in our yard, across the street, and along Neck Farm Road.

As the seasons rolled on, however, those who live on the island began to notice fewer deer. Where were the deer that usually nibbled the March lily growth in the front garden? Where were the fawns in June? At the post office, on the ferry, and wherever people gathered on Prudence Island, we wondered—Where are the deer?

On November 30, 1997, a man from Bristol shot a "blondish-gray," fully-grown female coyote on the island. No one had ever reported seeing a coyote on Prudence before. We wondered where it had come from and whether or not it was the only one. John Canario, our conservation officer, told *Sakonnet Times'* reporters that it could be one explanation for the reduced number of deer in the herd, though he had noticed deer smaller than usual and some with malformed antlers.

The '97 hunting season brought in only eighty-three deer. At the urging of John Canario and Senator Karen Nygaard, the Department of Environmental Management ended the season a month early on December 15th.

A week later we enjoyed our first snow that stayed on the ground. It came in a wild wind, first as rain, then as huge flakes driven sideways. Wet snow coated the front of the house, the windows, the lawn and the roads.

An inch or two of wet snow remained in some places when Matt and I walked down the dirt road leading east from our house to Neck Farm Road. Just as we reached the first clump of trees and bushes, Matt noticed what looked like huge dog prints and another set of smaller dog prints. The larger print contained five segments and measured more than three inches by three. We knew the size could have been augmented by the melting process. The animals had crossed over the road from the bushes on one side to the taller growth of trees and bushes on the other. Ordinarily, no dogs run loose in the area.

I drew in my breath as we noticed another set of foot prints crossing over the road, too. These prints were made by shoes or boots. "Do you think someone's hunting?" Matt asked.

"Kind of scary, don't you think?" I replied. Hunting season had been over for nine days. We didn't talk about it again. I thought someone's dogs might have gotten loose. That used to happen to us years ago when we had a dog that liked to wander away. We'd ride around the north end calling and calling, searching and searching.

The next night was one of those dead calm nights. When I came home from the post office, I walked out to the embankment and listened to the utter quiet. No tug boat engine sounded from afar. No night bird peeped. No dog barked. Matt and I continued working on Christmas gifts until dinner. He was making frames for pictures; I was making baskets. We went to bed around 9:30 p.m.

Just after midnight I awoke to sounds like women talking. Shaking out of my dream world, I realized that this was close to impossible. No one lives near us, nor would anyone be walking near our house in the dark of night, except in the event of an emergency.

I listened more closely and smiled at the yip, yip, yipping of what I thought might be two dogs. At first I thought that I was hearing one of my neighbors' dogs, either a half mile east of us or a mile northwest. Sometimes on still nights we hear an occasional bark in the distance. But this was too close and it was a different kind of bark.

The yipping was close, then farther away, then way in the distance, back closer, closer, then off fading into the distance, until it finally disappeared. What do foxes sound like when they are in pursuit? What do coyotes sound like? And what of the boot prints in the snow?

At the window I peered toward the road illuminated by our single street light, and I listened hard. But nothing moved and nothing made a sound near or far.

Time has passed and no one knows for sure why the deer herd suddenly plummeted and why for two years we saw far fewer deer than ever before. Some speculate that a major poach occurred after the 1997 hunting season. What other explanation could there be? Some of us became sleuths for a time but found no carcasses to indicate coyote or other fawn predators or to suggest disease as the culprit.

This springtime in the year 2000 we are seeing a blossoming of the herd. Yearlings browse. Pairs of fawns gambol across the dusty road.

"Lots of deer this year."

"Yup. Not what it was before, though."

"No, but the herd's growing again."

"Guess we'll never know what really happened."

On the island most mysteries are probed and solved at the ferry dock or wherever neighbors gather to share information and opinions, but the 1997 decline of the herd may go down in history as one unsolved mystery on Prudence Island.

10 | Lost: One Pie

By Josie Avery

One weekend Ann was off island with her kids.
They drove to Massachusetts to visit her parents. When it
was time to leave, her parents handed Ann a lovely frozen
blueberry pie from their larder. Arriving home on the 6 a.m.
ferry, Ann walked to her car with her two kids, two overnight bags, three grocery bags, and one bag with the
blueberry pie. She placed the bag containing the pie on the
roof of the car, and she loaded the kids and the rest of bags
into the car.

History would show that the pie stayed on top of the
car for about fifty feet before it fell onto the ferry parking
lot.

As she unpacked her groceries Ann realized the pie was
missing. At 8:15 a.m. the school bus pulled up, Ann stepped

onto the bus with her daughter and told Pat, the driver, about her pie. Pat said she saw a bag on the road down by the dock. At this point, Ann was hopeful. She got into the car and followed the bus.

Pat drove the bus into the parking lot, Ann behind her. As Ann helped a child step off the bus, she spied the pie. She waited as the child boarded the ferry, then turned to retrieve the pie. Just at that moment a young woman reached down, picked up the bag with the pie, peeked in and put the bag into her truck. The island police officer pulled up beside the young woman. He pointed to the bag and they nodded their heads in some sort of agreement. She handed the bag to the police officer, who then approached the highway department truck and showed the driver the bag. He looked into the bag, then up at the police officer, and shook his head.

Later that day, Ann's husband, who had heard the story of the pie, decided to have some fun. He called the police officer. "I'd like to report a missing pie," he said. Teary-eyed, Ann laughed in the background. The family had blueberry pie for dessert that night.

Keeping track of the stuff we load on and off the ferry requires a kind of honor system, as do many of the arrangements we make in our lives. We are shocked when someone "walks off" with a tote bag or shopping cart or case of beer. If we arrive home with an extra bundle of unidentified clothes or groceries, we immediately take the package down to Marcy's store where she will hold the goods for the rightful owner. Eventually owner and package are reunited. Sometimes a bundle takes a side trip to Hog Island on the summer service schedule but most everything arrives at the appropriate destination—like Ann's pie. That's the island way.

Sunset Hill Farm

11 | Planting Peas

by Grace Hall McEntee

It was only March 5th, but I had already turned over the soil on a small plot in our garden, here on Prudence Island. My husband Matt pounded two five-foot posts into the ground, and I attached wire fencing between them. At first this was simply preparation. I thought I might be able to wait until the following weekend to drop peas into the ground. It made more sense to wait. One year on April 10th a blizzard dropped temperatures to ten degrees.

The sun shone warmly on the south side of the house. For two weeks midday temperatures had risen above fifty degrees. Daffodils proclaimed springtime by reaching three inches above the ground.

Their buds swelled. The soil was dark, rich, and ready. I made my decision to plant.

Poking a row of inch-deep holes along the fencing on one side, then on the other, I tore open the fat seed packet at the corner and poured out a handful of hard peas. My left hand held peas and my right hand planted them.

One by one each seed dropped into its hole. Soil loosely cradled the seed, covered it, and became firm. My thoughts moved inside the seed to imagine how it would shift and change during the next seven to ten days. The tamped-down soil held my handprints, just as our concrete doorstep holds footprints of children, who claimed that this was their place to grow.

After I planted that day, our neighbor Jack Marmaras from the south end came by. He said, "Oh, I see you've planted peas. Me, too. I threw some of last year's in. Just to see what would happen." Then another neighbor Nate Bacon was on the phone and I said, "Yes, I planted my peas. I know it's early." Mid-island neighbors Al and Ann Hibbard have safely and sensibly begun hundreds of seeds indoors in their new greenhouse. I heard through the grapevine, though, that they planted spinach outdoors on February 2nd.

Four days after planting, the night temperature here in Rhode Island dropped to twenty-five degrees. I covered the cold frames in blankets, but I didn't cover the pea patch. Last night the temperature dropped to fifteen degrees. On the news I heard that Georgia peach growers fear that they have lost their entire crops. They fear financial disaster. For those of us who garden on Prudence Island, it's not that at all. If our little crops fail, we simply plant again ... and again.

Still, I will feel a twinge of regret if my germinating seeds freeze and fail. It has nothing to do with personal failure, more to do with caring about things that grow.

Soon Eddie Kuzis, another mid islander, will be back from Florida. I'll see him at Marcy's store and I'll ask Eddie, "How's your spinach?" He'll say it's "already this high," and demonstrate with his hands. As he talks he will become animated and he will smile. You can tell that Eddie cares about his garden. Maybe he plants his spinach in the fall before he leaves. I'll have to ask.

Then he'll ask, "How are your peas, Grace?" I'll answer in one of two ways. "Well, Eddie, I planted a little too early. They froze in the ground," or "They're terrific. They got an early start this year."

We make choices. My decision to plant early was partly the seduction of warm sun and loose soil but also partly exerting my own right to decide. Colder weather had been predicted. I decided I would plant while it was warm. When the warmth returned, the seeds might sprout. It was a calculated risk.

Here on the island when we meet neighbors in the springtime, we reconnect to each other and to the earth. We talk about choices and risks and caring—through our stories about planting peas.

12 | Prudence Island, A Place for Me

by Grace Hall McEntee

After a hot dusty ride along a rocky dirt road, nine of us—family and friends aged six to sixty—arrived at the house for sale. Surrounding the house, a field of bronze grass swayed in the ninety-degree August heat. Bees buzzed around wildflowers which grew near a '54 Chevy melting into the hot grass. We waded through knee-deep grass and flowers to peer through cracks in boarded windows. Darkness stared back at us.

We worked our way, wading and peering, to the front of the house. There, before us lay the cool bay. Without question or conversation, down the rickety steps to the rocky beach we hurried, shedding our shirts and shorts along the way. As nine bodies slid into the water, a communal sigh rose up, and we raised our eyes to give thanks. Imagine our shock when we saw two elderly ladies sitting on a bench at the top of the hill, watching. We elected Matt, still clothed in his running shorts, to climb the hill and act as a diversion. While he chatted, we crept out of the water and slid into our clothes.

And so we arrived at the place that would be our home. Prudence Island. Echoing another place further up Narragansett Bay where I had lived as a child, the sea scent, the light breeze, gulls screaming, the amniotic sea where I was spawned—all spoke to me. I had come home.

We removed the boards from the windows and brought sunshine into our new home. We broke through a wall to the east to welcome the morning sun and extended a room to the south to embrace the light of day. A new wing opens a view to the west. From there we savor twilight silhouettes of cedar and cherry against a backdrop of pink and red.

From our embankment, we watch in wonder as summer storms encircle the island, flashing a grand display of lightning and cloudbursts. Here we face winter's north wind and forge a strategy for our passage to and from the island as ice moves down the bay. We live in delicate balance with land and sea and with our neighbors, including the deer, loon, tick, cormorant, fly, swallow, fox, great blue heron, mink, gull, clam, and turtle.

For over twenty years we have lived on Prudence Island. For fifteen of them Matt and I commuted by boat from our island home to mainland jobs as educators. Now for four years Matt has commuted alone. Our work has demanded that we give of ourselves to children, their parents, and our colleagues. Our home at the edge of the embankment renews us. This island place manifests in a physical way that place of peace and light that I nurture within my mind.

Recently one serious morning before work, I jogged along that same dusty road that we had traveled with our group of nine so long ago.

My work was heavy on my mind. A giant snapping turtle emerged from the marsh at the crossroads. I don't ordinarily talk with turtles, but I felt compelled to speak with this beautiful creature, a grand survivor from ages past. "Hey, you handsome guy," I said. "Aren't you lucky to be able to stay on the island on this sunny day." He raised his gray-green head from his spiny shell and looked at me. I laughed and continued on home, where I showered and dressed for work. As I walked out the door to go to work, I smiled and realized that because of a turtle I'd met along the road, something in me had changed.

13 | *Phragmites* and the Sharp-tailed Sparrow

by Grace Hall McEntee

A tall young man in a tan visor hat walked out of the marsh at the crossroads. I had seen him and other young scientists working in the marsh. We had waved, but we were never close enough to speak.

"Hi, I'm Grace McEntee," I now said, holding out my hand.

He introduced himself as a former student at Brown, now at URI. We discussed people in both schools that we knew in common. Then I asked him to tell me about his work.

"I'm studying the sharp-tailed sparrow," he said. "It is not the sparrow that you ordinarily see around the island.

You would see the song sparrow. The sharp-tailed sparrow has a yellow patch on its cheek."

I pictured sparrows at my feeder—yellow on the head, yes, sparrows with no yellow, yes, yellow patch on the cheek, no.

He went on. "You probably wouldn't ever see the sharp-tailed sparrow since it hangs around the marsh, eating and nesting there. It is very secretive. When a marsh is disturbed it will leave. Here on Prudence we'll establish a baseline for the behavior of this bird.

"Some restoration work is being done at the marsh near Galilee, at the southern end of the state, where the causeway disturbed it years ago," he said.

"I remember when the causeway went in," I said.

"We are interested to know what will happen when the restoration work begins. Will sharp-tailed sparrows flock to Prudence for awhile until the work is done?" Prudence might be a desirable nearby habitat from the perspective of a dislodged sharp-tailed sparrow from Galilee.

Together we looked across the marsh. "See that reed on the other side of the marsh," he said. "That's called *phragmites*. It grows where humans have intervened. Sometimes it invades the natural growth. We hope to remove the *phragmites* from along the causeway at Galilee to restore the habitat for the sparrow."

I thought about the tall reed called *phragmites* with its tufted silhouette, clustered and swaying against the setting sun. Sometimes, on my way home from the post office as I drive past the town barn and swing onto the gravel road along the marsh, I stop to capture its beauty with my camera.

Field biologists study what happens when nature's critters and plants and humans bump up against each other in our world of limited space. Now, I have learned that the graceful *phragmites* invades the habitat of the secretive sharp-tailed sparrow.

Invasions will continue and studies march on.

And I will walk beyond the marsh toward home.

Marcy

14 | Bob and The Trail Gang

by Grace Hall McEntee

The blue truck stood by the side of the road, two wheels in the grass, two on the road. Farther on, a gray-haired man poked in the grass at papers and cans, hidden to most who pass by. He leaned into the job and lifted trash from the roadside.

"Good morning," I said, as I ran by.

"Good morning," he said.

"Who is that man in the blue truck?" I asked my husband one night.

"Oh, that's Bob Clachrie," he said.

Some visitors to the island fling beer cans from the windows of their cars or toss aside sweaty tissues as they ride bicycles along the dusty roads. Islanders routinely pick up trash where they walk. In all my years on the island, however, I have never seen anyone pick up trash along the roadside, day after day, as if his livelihood depended on it.

"Good morning, Bob," I now could say, as I ran by him.

"I put a picnic bench farther up in case you need to rest," he said one day. I laughed for the pure joy of hearing his words. Imagine someone saying that in the real world. It was hard to believe. Some days when I ran by he'd be mowing the grass near that picnic bench at Pulpit Rock.

During the fall when I was back in school, I ran in the afternoons and noticed new little trees, planted along the grass by the side of the road. Each sapling was carefully staked and fenced for protection against hungry white-tailed deer. Week after week more trees magically appeared. Maples, white pines, beech, a seemingly infinite variety— they became part of the landscape where I ran along Neck Farm Road, around the corner and up toward Apple Tree Beach, also know as Picnic Tree Beach. Now and then, like an elf caught stuffing a Christmas stocking, Bob would appear, shovel in hand, head perspiring, as I rounded the curve.

By this time Bob had a black truck. Some days I saw him with his wife Gerry, riding up to the north end to see the island in the light of the late afternoon sun. Other days I saw him with Al Corbett and John Butterworth in the truck. This was the beginning of the trail gang, and they were its charter members. Bob looked like a trail boss in his wide-brimmed straw hat. Al wore his baseball cap, and John his Greek fisherman's cap.

"Ah, he's sharing some of the good work," I thought to myself. But I was not really aware of the extent of the "good work" until some time later when I discovered that the crew was not only planting trees but also cutting through island bull briers to create walking paths.

"So people can get out and walk," Bob said one day. "So they won't have to worry about the ticks. Have you tried Sunset Trail?"

The "Trail Gang" is now a crew of sixteen or more. You'll recognize them by the sound of a mower or the sight of a shovel, and by the words "Trail Gang" on their work shirts. They clear and maintain miles of pathways, plant trees, and mow roadsides so that our island looks and feels like a carefully tended park. Their work includes the design, construction and mounting of birdhouses and the carving and installation of street signs so that the Fire Department can identify cross streets. And, of course, they collect beach trash. "We need more people to do this work," Bob said. "Leave the trash by the side of the road and we'll pick it up."

Over toward the west side, not far from Chase Way, a young maple stands more than fifteen feet tall. It no longer needs a fence, its leaves now beyond the reach of the deer. The work goes on. As of June 1998, not too long before Bob died, the Trail Gang had planted over two hundred trees and increased the number of species on the island by seven.

Years hence our children's children will stop to rest from biking over the hot and dusty summer roads. One of them might say, "Hey, let's go down that trail to see where it takes us," but first they'll rest in the shade of trees planted years before by the Trail Gang. They'll take out their map, more as a ritual than to actually see where they are heading.

And they might see printed on the bottom "Keep Prudence Island beautiful and accessible to all. Join the Trail Gang." They'll realize that somebody planted those trees and cut that path for them, and they might go on and do the same for others.

15 | Josie, Sunny Side Up

by Josie Avery

I was home recovering from an operation and wearing a spiker cast—it enclosed my trunk from chest to pelvis and extended down my left leg to my ankle. I could walk and lie down, but couldn't sit except when I used a specially modified stool that had half its seat carved out. Itchy, hot and bored, I thought, "This summer stinks!"

It was summer vacation and all the kids were riding their bikes, swimming, and taking trips with their families. I was stuck in my house on the first floor in a hospital bed watching TV and reading every teen magazine about the Beatles that I could get my hands on. Day after day the summer passed, until one day Mr. Harrington visited and said to my dad, "Josie is going on vacation!" He brought his station wagon over to our house, pushed down the back seat and loaded in a single bed mattress. He helped me into the back and off we went to the ferry and to Prudence.

I felt almost normal being back at Prudence. We arrived with the usual summer assortment of food and drink— way too much for even a big family to get through. By the second day, each child had diarrhea from eating red licorice. We were having a great time!

There wasn't much I could do that was different from my life at home but I felt good anyway. I couldn't sunbathe or swim but I followed everyone down to the beach. Standing, propped against my stool in the shade, I watched as my friend Sara and her brother and sister swam and played.

Even though I was careful not to venture too close to the water or get stuck in the sand, the inevitable happened and I fell. There I lay. My cast was so huge and bulky and heavy that not one of my friends or our mothers could budge me. I felt like a turtle flipped onto its back. Would I fry in the sun? Would I drown as the tide came in?

My friend Sara ran down the beach and found a willing and strong teenage boy. He slipped his arms around me and in a flash I was back on my feet. He was so cute. Smitten, I smiled. He sauntered off into the distance as my friends chimed, "Josie fell for Phil!"

Over the next several summers, Sara and I giggled and squealed every time we saw Phil. Behind her hand, Sara whispered "Josie fell for Phil."

16 | Growing Up and Growing Old

by Josie Avery

I have lived in the country, in the suburbs and in the "mother of all cities," New York. This confuses some people and so they ask, "Which do you prefer?" My answer is always the same, "I like the extremes." I would rather live in New York City or on Prudence Island than in Northampton, Massachusetts (and I have lived in all three places). Both of these places—Prudence and New York—have allowed me to experience a diversity of people that I would have missed in the suburbs.

Now that I am divorced, my family worries that I live in a place so far removed from the mainstream that I won't find a new mate. But I believe that life unfolds as it should and I am not fearful. Remembering my life in suburbia and in New York, I have found a community experience on the island that is different from life anywhere else. In other settings, I gravitate toward people who are a lot like me—those with similar jobs and education, the same social and economic background and of the same generation.

I've watched the kids grow up in the last eight years from toddlers on to kindergarteners at the island school and now as commuters to mainland schools. The island kids, like kids everywhere, need to fit in. Most times the children appear to be from one big family. I have watched them chide each other, laugh together and stick up for one another. If living on an island can be difficult for an adult, then the same must be said for the kids. Yet, island kids adapt, and I think learn early in life to be accepting of each other's differences.

It's hard to hide from adult eyes and judgments—there is no anonymity on an island. The adults have a certain relationship with the kids. We are more than just ambivalent onlookers or role models. Not a friend, not—for most—a relative, but something in between. We watch with concern, humor, consternation, and occasionally anger. As the children grow up, they know a childish mistake will not be overlooked but will be dealt with on the spot and maybe later a telephone call to home. Yet, this lack of anonymity can be a good thing—we heap attention on the kids for graduations, good report cards, new hairdos, and victories in sports. And oddly enough, the attention is reciprocated with interest in us—our lives, our happiness, and our mistakes.

Halloween is my favorite event with the kids. They split into two groups—the big kids and the little ones. The groups start at opposite ends of the island and trick or treat through the night. Sometimes they come by truck or sometimes on a hayride. Every year, it seems, the older kids arrive at my house after the little ones. They jump out of the truck and pile onto the porch. One boy, the same boy every year, waits to be last. As the other kids run back to the truck, he steps up to me, holds up his bag, and grins. "O.K., Josie," he says. And I pour the rest of the bowl into his bag. Every year, I plan for an invasion. He knows me well. I know him better.

On Prudence I stay connected to older people. Directly behind me in an old-style cottage my friend Grandma Bennett stays every summer. She has been coming to the island since she was a young girl. Grandma and her husband built their cottage in the 30's, in the usual island style using materials gleaned from elsewhere and patched together for over sixty years.

For as long as I have known her, Hildred Bennett has always been "Grandma." Every year Grandma and her daughter discuss whether or not it's wise for her to stay on the island by herself for three months. She is now ninety-two years old. Grandma says to me, "I tell her not to worry because Josie lives right in front of me." But I worry about her because I'm away all day, every day, working in the city and I'm often gone for weekends or overnights. I don't know how I feel about such responsibility.

On the island, Grandma experiences a freedom that she can no longer have in the winters, living as she does with her daughter in the city. Here she can get up and walk her little dog down to the dock to get a paper or the mail. She drove a car on the island until last year but this summer she stopped because her vision began to fail.

She walks across the lawn and visits with her friend Mrs. Connors, who at ninety-five is one of the oldest island residents. They sit on the deck, look out over the bay and chat. Because they are both going deaf, they talk so loudly that it's hard not hear every word when they review *my* daily routine.

At night when Grandma watches "Jeopardy," I can turn down the volume on my set and hear every question and every answer. I always know what time it is by the game show theme songs pouring out of Grandma's television set.

Grandma used to head down to the beach to dig her own quahogs but these days she can't make the stairs. I am not a very talented quahogger but some of my friends are. Whenever they give me quahogs, I share them with Grandma and watch her eyes smile. She looks at me and says, "Josie, I just love you!"

I am lucky to know people like Grandma Bennett whose experiences and sensibilities may not be the same as my own. Would I know her in a place bigger, busier, or noisier? By the same token, in a larger town or city would I be invited to Brownie Scout fly-up ceremonies or sit and debate the pros and cons of Macs versus PCs with teenage boys? We sit next to each other day after day on the ferry. We raise our hands in a "hello" driving down the road. We stop and talk about the weather. We speak to each other. We take the time. On the island, this is how we grow up and how we grow old.

Winter Shawl

17 | A Place Where Almost Everyone Counts

by Josie Avery

Traveling on the ferry the other day, I met an environmental scientist on his way to work at the south end of the island. He asked me how many people live here. I paused, then blurted, "One hundred fifty." But I was bluffing. Everyone gives a different number when it comes to estimating how many of us live on the island. I always say that there are about one hundred fifty of us in the dead of winter. But that's just a guess. A couple of years back I began to work on my own census, but I changed computers and lost the file.

I moved to the island in the fall of 1991. Now, I was "a year rounder," no longer a summer person. I became friendly with Ann and Bob Marshall, who had also recently moved here. During that first winter, we would get together and try to figure out "the island ways" of this place we now inhabited. Sometimes we tried to guess the number of islanders. Later we were fascinated to learn that two island women—each with her own criteria for qualification—kept a winter census.

I kept my mainland apartment in Bristol that winter and, for awhile, coasted back and forth enjoying the best of both worlds. Over the Christmas holidays I went out to Washington—as is my yearly ritual—and took my sweet time returning to the island. After all, it was cold.

At the beginning of the second week of January, I received the call that motivated my return to the island. "People are beginning to talk," my friend said, "If you don't get your ass back here, they'll take you off the census." I boarded the ferry the next day.

For seven winters now, my friend and I have watched people move on and off the island. We keep our own mental census and speculate as to who will make it and who will not—and whether or not we will. We are often wrong.

After my conversation with the scientist, I walked off the ferry and decided it was time to ask the one who would know—Marcy. "So, how many people *are* there on the island?" I said. Right off the top of her head Marcy said, "A hundred. Winter people." "Really," I said, "only a hundred? I thought for sure it was a hundred fifty. I started making a list a couple of years ago and I had a little over a hundred. Then I published the phone book and listed almost three hundred."

"I don't count a lot of people," Marcy said. "I don't count all those people who go to Florida or someplace on the mainland for the winter."

18 | A Dead Thing

by Grace Hall McEntee

The sun cast a pink veil over the deserted beach at twilight. The crescent shore cupped silver water. Bronze marsh grass rustled in the light wind. Except for swaying grass and rippling water, nothing moved.

Entering the beach from the path that leads through the bull briers and grape vines, I hesitated as always, breathed in the spectacle of the sea before me, looked left, then right toward the setting sun. There in the distance on the slope of the smooth sand, I saw a dark lump, its silhouette etched on this canvas, breaking the smooth line of the beach. The lump might have been an old tire, the hull of a tiny abandoned dinghy, a small barrel, a rounded rib of wood, or a dead thing.

I had grown up at the beach and had been there as a

child when rescuers searched waters for missing swimmers and when teams eventually dragged for bodies. From those days to this one, I have expected to find a body, either bobbing bloated in the water or half buried on the sandy beach. I considered the lump and wondered whether this would be the day. Neither dreading nor desiring the experience, I walked evenly toward what now seemed to be a body.

On October 26, 1985, Vinny and Elizabeth DeAndrade, two Prudence Island neighbors, failed to return to the island in their small plane. Volunteers searching in the fog the next morning turned up nothing. Later in the day when the fog had lifted, Tony DiBiasio—an "eye in the sky" pilot—spotted the submerged plane beyond the runway on the west side. Would-be rescuers found Elizabeth still strapped into her seat in the plane. Weeks later, I walked with my dog and my own ambivalence to the northwest corner of the island to see if the marsh grass was hiding Vinny's body. Three weeks later someone found his body there.

Now, I approached a dead thing on the beach. Face down it lay, like a large dark baby, sleeping. Lapping waves had washed soft sand over its head. Its upper limbs seemed more like arms than flippers. Skin folded softly in the crook of arms, bent at the elbow toward the head. Fingernails emerging from pale nail beds dug into the sand. "Definitely not a seal," I thought.

Smooth gray leathery skin stretched four or five feet

from the partially covered head to the outstretched toes. One small tuft of fur on the back hinted that the entire body had once been so covered. "Certainly not a human," I thought, though it seemed more human than animal, the way it was lying there.

I wanted to see its face, but when I reached to uncover it, some sense, perhaps of decorum, maybe something else, held me back. We cover our dead. Could I now uncover this face?

As a lay "scientist," I wanted to examine the bone structure of the skull, look at the jaw, count teeth, examine the eyes and ears, but I could not. It was not from any revulsion that I felt. Exactly the opposite. I was drawn to the thing. Yet I could not take the last step that would help me to know it better. So I left the dead thing lying there.

Back home I called John Canario, our conservation officer on the island, to report what I had seen on the beach. "John, I think it's a sea otter," I said.

As I uttered the words, a light flicked on in my mind, a memory from a class in which I was a student. As a pre-writing activity the instructor had asked us to choose an animal to serve as a metaphor for ourselves. Though I had never seen sea otters other than on television or in books and magazines, I knew them as playful and gregarious—sliding with friends over slippery rocks—as clever and comical—floating on their backs to crack open shellfish on their chests. I was a sea otter.

Years later on Sandy Beach at Prudence Island, a dead

thing lay, a sea otter washed ashore, arms wrinkled like a baby's, head hidden by soft sand. And I could not uncover its face.

19 | Rock and Roll

by Josie Avery

Prudence commuters dread those days when the winds are so high we cannot get to work, but even more we dread those nights when we cannot get back home. Around late October we pack a small overnight bag to leave in our cars. Personal hygiene items like shampoo and deodorants don't do well—through trial and error we learn what stuff can be left in a freezing car day after day. Likewise, when we are "stuck off island," we have learned to unpack our bags as soon as we reach a home base. We need to let the night's pajamas warm up a bit before we put them on.

Some days we get on the ferry and the winds are howling. On days like this we like to say, "Looks like we're in for a little rock and roll." We all have our "war stories" about our worst ride.

My worst ferry ride took place one November night shortly after the beginning of hunting season on the island. I marked the date because my dog Isis was sick from eating deer entrails thrown away by hunters. Taking her to the vet's had interrupted my day. By the time I reached the ferry I was cranky about the whole ordeal, the inconvenience, and the cost.

We set out from Bristol on the last boat. The fourteen-car ferry, known as the "big boat" was still in service. Most of the commuters sat in the single cabin, port side on the deck level and a couple of people went topside to the open deck. While I do not remember all of the passengers that night, I do recall Mark Goulet, Maria Civetti, Ann Marshall and her daughter Kit sitting in the cabin. As we got underway, I was telling those who would listen the gory details of my dog's illness from eating deer offal. Part way into the story, the wind blowing from the south picked up and the waves pummeled the bow.

Maria's face turned a particular shade of green. I knew that to keep Maria's friendship, I'd better shut up. Mark Goulet had dozed off. Kit and Ann had gone out on deck to feel the winds. In a moment, Ann returned looking very nervous and asked, "Where are we?"

I said, "How would I know? You were the one who was outside!"

Because of the darkness and the waves, it was impossible for her to tell where we were. No stars, no moon, no shoreline lights shone. The ferry pitched in the wind and waves, and we inside the cabin held onto our seats, eyeing the life jackets.

A very wet Chris Dunbar stumbled into the cabin. Topside for the ride, she had nearly gotten tossed over into the water. But the deckhand grabbed her jacket and pulled her into the wheelhouse.

The sudden change in weather—the south wind and the tide shift piling waves against the ferry—forced the Captain to make a decision. We would return to Bristol Harbor.

Usually, we are disappointed to be stuck off the island, but this time we happily accepted the prospect of spending an unplanned night in town—everyone except for Mark Goulet, who slept through the entire ordeal. Surprised to see the lights of Bristol—not the lights of Homestead Dock—he was heard to say, "When did we turn around?"

As I walked off the ferry, I heard a pinging and glanced over at the flags. They were flying straight out in the wind. Now on breezy days, I check the flags and wonder—is it time to rock and roll?

Prudence Island Ferry

20 | Glimpses of Island Life

by Josie Avery

It never fails. Whenever I tell people that I live on an island, they are charmed. As they begin to ask more questions, get a clearer picture of life on an island—accessible only by ferry—then they are not so sure if they envy me. Island life is certainly not for everyone. Often as I describe the island, people say that I must be a true isolationist. But that's not how I see life on the island.

People who live on islands are connected in many fundamental ways. On my island, Prudence, we wave to each other as we drive by. It's not a big enthusiastic wave—it's more like a nod. Each of us has our own distinctive wave—the hand barely rising from the steering wheel, the fingers wiggling, or the Queen Mum's. If there is one easy way to distinguish tourists from islanders, it is this—the wave.

We connect at "boat time." If I want to know what's happening or who's just come to the island, I go down to Homestead and meet the boat. Islanders hang out in front of Marcy's store or the post office. They are there just because it's "boat time." If someone shares a piece of island news with me and I question the source, they might simply say, "I heard it at the boat." This does not mean they heard it on the commute, it means they heard it at the dock, waiting for the boat, probably in front of Marcy's.

Homestead Dock is often a place of reunion. In the summer as people come off the boat, friends and relatives hug and share news of the past months. I remember standing at the dock one day, watching two childhood friends greet each other. As one came off the ferry she yelled to her friend who was boarding, "Hey, where ya going?"

"To the hospital. I'm in labor," she said.

On weekends, if I'm sitting on my friend's porch, we watch the island drive by on its way to and from the dump. We may spot a chair or a table in the back of a truck and wonder whose house it will grace at the end of the day. When I go to the dump, I usually get some help with my garbage bags from whoever is on duty. We exchange a bit of news and always talk about the weather. People stand around and admire the woodpile or the cast-offs—bikes, old lawn furniture, gas grills, baskets, baby strollers and once a mannequin. Often they leave with a "new" table. Islanders are true believers in recycling.

Island life is not about isolation. Your presence or

absence is noted when you live in a place as small as our island. The lights at your house are out, your mail and Sunday papers pile up, your lawn is unruly and we notice. We notice when your temper is short, your cough lingers, your spirits are sagging. We notice you've shaved your beard, you look good in blue and whose truck was parked in your driveway overnight.

The Stores

Fredy's Fruit Store

It was the third week of December and I drove by Fredy's Fruit Store, which was closed for the season. I looked into the big sliding glass window and noticed the sign thanking us for our business was not visible. I hoped it was not an omen. Fredy's return is an unofficial signal that summer has begun.

Fredy and his wife Evelyn—also known as Mrs. Fredy— did return that year. By the Memorial Day weekend, they were in full swing, greeting customers and filling orders, but there was something different. In the middle of the store stood an easel upon which Fredy and Evelyn had placed a list of islanders who had died. It was their gift to the island on that Memorial Day weekend.

Seeing it reminded me of the fragility of our community. I read through the names and pointed out to Fredy a few that were missing. Throughout the weekend and into the next week, islanders read slowly through the names. Some added to the list. Others were pleased to see their people remembered. Fredy and Evelyn had performed a valuable service.

Fredy's store is a wonder of design. When you first enter the store, it's hard to know where to look. To the immediate left of the entryway is a bulletin board with business cards, announcements and sign-up sheets, and at the bottom is a bumper sticker that always used to make my husband and me laugh. It says "Married but not dead." Above the bulletin board on the wall is a clock made from an avocado-colored toilet seat that says Fredy's Fruits on it. I never quite understood why anyone would want to make a toilet seat into a clock, but it must have made sense to someone.

The rich smell of fresh produce draws the eye to the center aisle filled with baskets of whatever is in season— onions, tomatoes, zucchini, peaches, cherries—all carefully arranged. An old-fashioned scale hangs from above prompting customers to weigh the items they select.

Each year Fredy and Evelyn have continued to expand their selection of fresh fruits and vegetables to accommodate the island. If you want only two ears of corn, then that's what Fredy will sell you. If you get to the store and there are no more mushrooms, Fredy will say, "Oh, I just sold the last box to Bob Marshall." I'll laugh and say, "I wonder what time they're having dinner?" As if I could just drop in and have some of those mushrooms.

My friends from New York City experience sensory overload when they go to Fredy's. I'm not sure if it's Fredy's or Evelyn's personality or the layout of the store itself. My friend Gail brought out her camera during one visit and started clicking away. She needed proof. No one in New York would believe her description. Her favorite part of the store design is the propped refrigerator door used to display health and beauty aids as well as feminine hygiene products.

Deano's Country Store

Olivia and John Canario own and run Deano's Country Store. We call it "Canario's." Outside, John Canario has fashioned birdhouses and signs—original folk art. Signs admonish observers to be quiet as Mrs. Wren and her brood are sleeping. Other birdhouses are named—a "quilters village," a "honeymoon cottage" and even a "Birds' Bates Motel, Rooms for the Nite. No reservations needed. You will rest in peace." Still another sign announces: " Square Dancing every Saturday. Caller: Mr. Red Cardinal. Music by the Mocking Birds. Admission: 10 worms + 5 beetles." On the lawn is a menagerie of swans and pink flamingoes. Reindeer fly and a hobbyhorse leaps from the shrubbery. The trees are laden with plastic fruit.

On a more serious note, a small sign reads—"Notary Public." Beside the steps a bulletin board carries announcements about wildlife and island events.

The small store adjoins their kitchen and the aroma of

cooking permeates the air. The place is packed with all manner of goods. Every square inch of space is used for canned goods, bread, candy, announcements, and the Prudence Island Quilters' cookbook, entitled *Our Sea-Cret Recipes*. Brochures about ticks, Lyme disease and deer hunting lie on the counter.

As the island conservation officer and "doctor of wildlife," John Canario has a keen interest and knowledge of our plants and animals. A couple of weeks ago I mentioned to John that I had seen a blue heron. I described how the huge gray bird flew above my truck as I wound my way towards the neck of the island. "Yes," he said, he'd seen the bird. "Actually," he said, "there are three of those birds out there but I haven't said anything to anyone because I don't want them disturbed. They can be very sensitive when they are breeding." I understood that John expected me to keep this information to myself.

Marcy's

If Marcy's store has an official name, by now everyone has forgotten it. Once, someone designed a T-shirt with Horace Barrett's illustration of Marcy's and the words "The Prudence Island Mall." Everyone laughed, but the name didn't stick. "I gotta go to Marcy's," you say, and everyone knows where you are headed. They know you are going to the store and not dropping by to visit Marcy at home.

Over the years, Marcy's store has been a natural gathering place for islanders. Even before Bob Clachrie made a beautiful new bench for outside the store, milk crates and planks of wood served as makeshift benches. As goods and mail arrive on the ferry, customers and friends pitch in to help Marcy bring them into the store. Someone might head out onto the ferry with a two-wheeler hand truck to carry off the milk or ice cream.

Marcy's is the repository of lost and misplaced bundles and packages. When someone heads home with the wrong groceries, they bring them to Marcy's store. At any moment Marcy is likely to get a call asking if anyone has found a bag of groceries or if Uncle Joe got off the boat.

On Sunday morning islanders gather at the 10:30 a.m. boat for their papers. The ritual is always the same—after the vehicles and passengers leave the boat, someone backs a car or truck onto the ferry to load the Sunday editions. The papers are driven up to the side of the porch and taken into the store where islanders line up by the counter, waiting. Marcy and a helper assemble all the *Providence Journals* dispensed at the cash register. In the middle of the store, subscribers to the *New York Times* and the *Boston Globe* assemble their own papers.

Marcy stocks a variety of goods at her store: fresh milk and baked goods, canned goods, cookies, locally published books, jewelry and crafts, as well as cleaning products, mousetraps and the ever practical cans of Fix-a-Flat. She relies on her customers to be reasonably self sufficient and honest. A gas pump stands behind the store. Marcy gives instructions on how to pump the gas. After that—unless they truly require assistance—customers are on their own.

Shopping, the Prudence Way

Shopping for food is a serious business for most of us, but particularly for islanders. In the summer, three stores on the island cater to the day-to-day small grocery needs of islanders and tourists. In the winter there are only two. Whatever the season most islanders do their "big" shopping off island. We take the gathering of provisions seriously—no late night runs to a 24-Hour Super Stop & Shop or 7-11. We must be prepared for most situations. Grocery shopping is not a capricious undertaking—it takes planning and organization. This is why islanders have in their homes large freezers and why they belong to warehouse shopping clubs.

To convey supplies on and off the ferry, islanders use contraptions including two-wheelers, bicycle-shopping cart combinations, and all manner of tote bags, milk crates, carts, wagons, back packs and trash cans on dollies.

On Wednesdays retirees shop during the four hours between the 10:30 and the 3:30 boats. This leaves them with enough time to grab a quick lunch after shopping, maybe go to a doctor or dentist appointment and get back to the boat. Some refer to this day as "going to America!"

Commuters usually shop on Thursday, anxious to get their sacks and full carts on and off the boat without having to compete for space with weekenders. Shoppers handle their bags of groceries several times from store to home—from the store to the car, car to the ferry, ferry to the island car, and island car to the home. Finally, shoppers put away their groceries.

Even when it's not a shopping day, everyone carries something on and off the ferryboat. When my brother and I were kids, my mother and father made it clear to us that we were never to leave the ferry empty handed. Chances were that if our family had nothing to carry, someone else could probably use our help.

When I was a summer person, getting all my stuff onto the boat seemed a major undertaking. Well trained by my mother, I made a bag and bundle count at least three times during the half-hour ride. Now that I am a resident, I am a little less obsessive and a little more in control.

I have lost only one bundle in the past ten years. One New Year's Eve a bag containing a half-gallon of orange juice and a bottle of champagne was delivered to the ferry. I had told my friend to put my name on the bag. There was an unusually low moon tide that night, and the ferry could not tie up to the dock. Against the backdrop of the illuminated Mount Hope Bridge, commuters became revelers, cruising the bay. When the ferry pulled up to the dock a few hours later, I went on board but found no bag. Maybe they drank a toast to me. I hope so.

ferry landing   Post Office   bulletin board   General Store   island phone   island gas

·PRUDENCE ISLAND MALL·

21 | Time Well Spent

by Josie Avery

Today I sat down with my calculator to figure out how long I spend commuting in one year. A round-trip ferry ride takes one hour. I commute to work five days a week. I work forty-eight weeks a year. So,

> 5 hours x 48 weeks =240 hours per year or ten full
> days—just commuting to work.

What I do with my time on the boat varies from day to day, week to week. I might sit and talk with my neighbors to catch up on the news. I might seek out other passengers for information. Who is the best contractor? Who gives the best deal for loam?

Tonight I rode over on the boat with my neighbor

Melanie and caught up on her news. Melanie and Gene are my closest neighbors during the winter, but we don't often have a chance to socialize. They are the consummate commuters. He travels to his job in Connecticut while she works for a company based in Ohio. Sometimes we holler "Hello!" or "How ya doin'?" to each other across a dirt road and our yards. We visit from time to time, but it has been several months since she and I have sat down just to catch up. Now we know each other's holiday plans, and she will keep an eye on my house while I travel west for Christmas. This kind of "visiting" happens a lot on the ferry.

Besides talking, reading is the second most popular pastime on the boat. There is a natural order of selection in reading the morning *Providence Journal*. I always want "Lifebeat " which contains the horoscope, Ann Landers and celebrity gossip. Morning is not my highbrow part of the day. Shannon and Dan read the sports, and they hand Matt the business section. Andrew Porter and Barbara Bacon take the front section. Later Barbara will share news and obituaries with me from the metro section. Several people work on the crossword puzzle.

Books also make the rounds on the boat. Occasionally, someone will ask me what I am reading or I might tell someone, "You'd really like this book." After eight years of commuting on the boat I know who reads mysteries, who reads romances and who likes Irish history. My fellow commuters also know my preferences.

The ferry cabins often serve as temporary office space.

Kids on their way to and from school hunch over schoolbooks and reports in an effort to start or finish homework. In the last two years, cell phones have made their appearance and occasionally I hear the sound of the gentle tapping of laptop keys. I use my time on the ferry to pay bills. Writing out checks is an onerous task but it makes me feel virtuous.

Some days I think of the ferry as a kind of mobile consumer report. Passengers are always giving each other advice about where to get the best deal or how to make the best selection. If there is a deal to be had, Prudence Islanders know where to go. Advertisements and coupons are crammed into our briefcases, purses and pockets. Armed with advice from our fellow travelers, off we go to shop. Then, with pride we haul our booty onto the ferry, where someone will lean over and look into the box or bag and say, "Hey, where'd you get that?"

The funniest memory I have of consumer advice is the day I was instructed on how to pick out a good brassiere. I was sitting in the smoking cabin on the morning boat heading for Bristol with three other women. Somehow we got onto the subject of how to buy a "good bra." One of the women said, "Never buy a bra with only two snaps in the back, always get one with three. They give more support." Her friend leaned over to demonstrate the scooping motion you must use in order to put a bra on and get a good fit. By the time we arrived in Bristol we were howling with laughter at the absurdity of our conversation, grateful that no man had ventured into our cabin girl talk.

The ferry takes us from the mundane in our lives to the extraordinary. Once in awhile the ferry bears mourners, flowers and an urn of ashes. It brings the remains of the ones we love to be cast with flowers upon the waters of Narragansett Bay. It takes us home.

22 | The Family Clambake

by Grace Hall McEntee

Celebratory feasts have a long tradition. They form anchors for a year, points of stability between willy-nilly activities. Stories arise from these traditional feasts. They tap into collective memory and build upon it. They bind us together. For our small community of family and friends, one such feast is the McEntee family clambake.

In our albums, clambake photos all look pretty much the same. Matt's brothers Mike, Ed and O and Matt's son Mattie have boats anchored in front of our house. Tire tubes—bobbing in the water—cradle his sister Beth and his brother's friend Helen. Matt's brother Brian and the children water ski. Mother McEntee and Claire—our elders—sit at the top of the embankment, watching. As we turn the pages spanning two decades, we notice that the children clearly change over the years while the adults seem to remain the same. (This is not entirely true, but for the sake of the narrative, I'll go on) It is in the storytelling, that each clambake is defined.

One lightly sprinkled comment can trigger a memory. Trumpets blare and a brightly colored flag unfurls, displaying the image from that particular year. On one flag, for example, the image of a northeast wind howls. That was the year of the wind. On another, a single lobster— representing the many—holds a freedom flag. On a third, one winged fork tickles our memory.

I am the tribal scribe. My duty is to record what we have learned in my clambake log. The night before the bake as our family sits together to plan, I read aloud from the record of our lessons learned.

The Year of the Wind

Our phone call to family and friends about the upcoming August clambake inspires conversation and gustatory remembrances of savory clam chowder, tasty fish bags, tender lobster, sweet succulent corn, and delectable potatoes. We hold the annual bake on the rocky shore of the north-facing beach, below the embankment in front of our house.

Early on the morning of the bake, a few volunteers dig a foot-deep pit in the sand. My daughter and her husband, a former engineer and a design carpenter, respectively, take charge of this operation. "Last year's pit was a little too big," Laurie might say to Jim. Her hands are on her hips and she is smiling. Having learned about pits and cribs from study and experience, they mean to make this right. Jim pulls his measuring tape from the pocket of his jeans and measures the one they have dug—"Ah! 3' x 3'. Perfect," he says, in a deep voice sifting through his beard and mustache.

At the top of the embankment Matt pulls the cord on the chainsaw and rough cuts wood collected from the beach and from the dump. After he has created a hefty pile, he calls in a raucous voice, "Ready?" He clowns for the audience below and tosses wood to the pit location where Mattie manages the collecting of materials. Matt sets up hoses for controlling the pit fire. His son with a crew on the beach gathers rocks the size of a man's head. Along with the wood, they place the rocks close to the pit for the construction of the crib.

Standing face to face, hands gesturing and arms pointing, or squatting like two children at play, Laurie and Jim plan the crib, a structure meant to be burned. The past informs the present. They recall lessons learned from other cribs that leaned, then fell to one side or the other as they burned. They set about the task of constructing the crib, alternating wood and rocks, building layer upon layer. Last year the crib became an eight-foot pyramid.

At this point, Matt, Mattie, and his helpers, along with Laurie and swimmers who have gathered on the beach all come to attention. The crib is finished. Those on the hill focus their cameras. Jim squats close to the crib, ignites a match and holds it to newspapers he has quickly read then stuffed under the first layer of wood. On a good day, the paper ignites and the fire quickly roars to a bonfire. Swimmers dive back into the water. Those atop the hill sit down and continue their conversations.

The burning of the wood heats the rocks, which eventually fall into and fill the pit. Leftover rocks and ash are raked away. The hot rocks covered with a layer of seaweed provide steam for cooking. The goal—to achieve a perfect bake.

During the year of the wind, however, while the crib *did* burn and collapse as planned, a steady twenty-five knot northeast wind blew the heat to the southwest side of the bake. That side cooked to perfection, while the other emerged like a Prudence Island raw bar. My chowder, steamers, and salad—all prepared safely away from the pit—were a big hit that year.

Henceforth, at the first puff of a north wind, we erect a wind break—a dinghy tipped on its side or a piece of old plywood retrieved from the island transfer station.

The Year of the Lobster

Matt prefers to purchase lobsters on the morning of the bake, but that poses a dilemma since he is needed for wood cutting and pit preparation. After all, he is—at least in theory—the bake master. So the afternoon before the bake, he often zooms off in the boat to Barrington or to Warwick to buy lobsters. This early pickup poses a challenge—how to keep the lobsters fresh. Having learned that we could not keep the lobsters overnight in a dinghy full of sea water (They all died that year), the next year we decided to keep them in a lobster trap attached to our pulley line in front of the house. We felt confident the lobsters were safe.

At low tide on the day before the annual bake we gather rockweed—a type of seaweed . My nephew Michael, Matt, and I, along with two friends, picked up thirteen string quahog bags—like huge onion bags—and climbed into the back of the truck for the ride to the west side of the island. Dust swirled as the truck bounced and rattled along the dirt road. At Halfway Rock, where the rocky shore is close to the road, we descended to search for rockweed. Under the shadows cast by the afternoon sun, we squatted like ancient gatherers and pulled rockweed—handful by handful—until we had filled our thirteen bags.

On the day of a bake after the wood has burned, the crib has collapsed, and the rocks have fallen into the pit— hot and ready to cook—we spread a six-inch deep layer of rockweed over the hot rocks. Half the rockweed lies under the bake and half over it to form a natural steamer for the food.

During the year of the lobster, steam rose from the first layer of rockweed, producing hot sea scents. Workers salivated as they reached into baskets for lightly oiled potatoes individually wrapped in foil and corn still in its husk. They leaned over the pit and laid them on the bed of steaming seaweed. Then, ever so carefully, they picked up fish bags—brown lunch bags containing scrod, sausage, hot dog, a carrot and an onion—and laid them on top of the potatoes and corn. The bake was ready for the lobsters.

Hand over hand, Matt hauled the lobster crate in from the pulley line and dragged it onto the rocky beach. There where the water meets the shore he counted and then recounted. He shook his head and counted once again. Only fifteen of the thirty lobsters remained in the crate. Half of them had escaped! Chagrined, we set the remaining lobsters on the bake and placed the test potato on top.

While the bake steamed under the tarp on the beach, we feasted on chowder, mussels, steamers, salad, and homemade bread. After an hour, as usual, we tested the potato and unloaded the bake. During part two of the feast we heard cries of delight. "This is wonderful!" "Cooked to perfection!" Under tarps and between two layers of rockweed, the bake had steamed into one of our best. No one mentioned the fifteen lobsters that had escaped.

But when the ferry had long since departed and when the wakes of brothers' boats were no longer visible, we gathered up leftovers and discovered a miracle that year. Not fishes and loaves, but lobsters left over! Brothers had left theirs for brothers, friends for friends.

The Year of the Fork

Other clambakes, too, remain in our memory for one incident or another. None will go down in history with such a vivid recollection as a recent clambake that has come to be known as the year of the fork.

At first I thought it would be remembered as the year of the deluge. On Friday night, weather forecasters predicted heavy downpours for that Saturday morning with clearing in the afternoon. We decided to wait until morning to make our decision about whether to reschedule—keeping steamers, lobsters, and rockweed fresh is the looming challenge with a postponement. That night rain pounded heavily against the north-facing windows. Thunder and lightning performed fireworks and led us to the hope that the storm would pass. And indeed, on Saturday morning, we awoke to azure skies and puffy white clouds. We fielded calls and made as many, adjusting and readjusting plans. The forecast still called for thunderstorms and heavy downpours, but we thought it might be a "left over" forecast. The sky was, after all, blue.

The weather seemed perfect for the clambake. Guests arrived by truck, in their own boats and by ferry. Mattie's two friends zoomed down from the upper bay in their inflatable raft.

People sat around preparing food—peeling carrots, folding fish bags, and scraping mussels—for steaming. Clouds gathered as we were about to load the bake, and the skies poured a torrent onto the rockweed covering the hot rocks. As if it came up from the bubbling core of the earth, thick steam rose from the pit. Hands appeared out of the steam, reached into the center, and dropped corn or a fish bag onto the bake. Disembodied voices called out, "No more corn here." "We've finished with fish bags here." "We're ready for the lobsters."

Our clothes stuck to our skin as we carefully laid lobsters on the bake. Even in the steam we shivered as the testing potato was placed ceremoniously on top. We drew the heavy canvas over the bake and sealed the edges with rocks.

In the yard, committees of workers erected nylon tarps for the protection of our outdoor party. A huge green tarp, stretched over the picnic table, promptly filled with water and split, sending gallons of water spilling onto those sitting under it. To replace it, our friends Jack and Rosemary raced home in their red truck to get an old sail. So it seemed that this clambake would be known as the year of the deluge.

But an incident occurred which overrode the deluge in historical memory, particularly for those of us who enjoy a periodic chuckle at our own expense. After the bake had been on for an hour, we prepared to check the single unwrapped potato, placed on the top of the bake as the tester. We know that when the fork easily pierces the potato, the bake is done.

Someone from the beach yelled up. "Send down the fork!" Mattie's two friends were sitting on their inflatable raft in the rain, talking with guests. Others were hosing the periphery of the bake to keep the outer edges of the tarps from igniting—a possibility even in the rain. "Heads up. Here it comes," the fork messenger said from atop of the embankment. Mattie's friends moved from their raft, back toward the water. Everyone stood alert, heads up.

The fork flew from the top of the hill. Those who reported later swore that in its flight the fork seemed to assume a mind of its own. Then they heard, "Thunk!" They turned their heads this way and that, in search of the errant fork. "Ssssssss." A ripple of dismayed laughter washed over those on the beach. There, still quivering from its landing, was the fork—firmly implanted in the previously inflatable raft. Amazed, we watched as the raft slowly folded in upon itself.

That bake will not go down in the annals of McEntee clambake history, as the clambake of '97 or as the year of the deluge. We will remember it as "the year of the fork," and we'll chuckle as we continue to craft the story of this celebratory feast.

Scallop

23 | Leave Taking

by Josie Avery

"Michael's leaving," I say, dropping my voice as I speak to Ned, a mainland friend who has ties to the island. I feel foolish trying to describe how we islanders feel when one of us moves "off," at a loss to describe the type of bond islanders share with one another—even with those people we barely know. In this instance, Michael is a friend.

Still others are leaving our island this fall, a family of seven I do not know well. Yet I realize that this family will leave a hole in the fabric of our community among schoolchildren, men and women who fish for sport and the gatherings at their home for Saturday morning calamari making. Here on the island, everyone's presence matters.

When the rumors abound about new people moving here, we joke about the application process and a call for references. We wish to know how this family or individual will affect—both physically and socially—the delicate balance of our community.

Islanders tend to be cautious about new people. Establishing a social niche can be a slow process, and it seems the harder you try, the more elusive your station becomes. Maybe it's that New England attitude—holding back, keeping our secrets. Maybe it's the recognition that life can be difficult here and that you may not stay. We are not sure how much of our time or how much of ourselves we should invest. We wait for you to prove your mettle. After all, winters can be bleak and the isolation overwhelming. We wonder—can you make it through the winter?

I remember seeing Michael when he first moved to the island five years ago. As with most new people, my friends and I wondered, "Who *is* that?" As it turned out, Michael was Grace McEntee's nephew. A prior connection to the island and its people always gives the newcomer a certain "in." We feel better when we know who your people are, who you belong to.

We invested a lot in Michael, and he in us. I think about his decision to go—*his leave taking*. It will upset the balance of our community. He leaves with a wealth of our secrets. Watching Michael drive the Ryder truck onto the ferry this past Sunday, I knew our secrets were safe in his keeping.

Acknowledgments

Thank you to all who have helped us along the way. Among those who sat with us to tell stories were Ann Hibbard and Bill Bisordi, but their stories did not make their way into this collection. Still they were part of the conceptualization of what *Home At Last* would be.

Friends on and off the island reviewed our first draft. They were Al Hibbard, Alison Townsend, Matt McEntee, Joe Bains, Irene Travis, Christine Dunbar, Laurie Freeman, Jim Strickland, and Michael Crowley. We took their comments to heart and revised. When our stories seemed as "finished" as they could be, Joel Maguire, Rachel Smith, Lynne Antaya Mingin, and Bill Bisordi read them aloud so we could hear the flow of our prose. And we revised. Then we gave the manuscript to Jane Maguire for a thorough reading. From Jane it went to Ann Marshall, our trusted island friend and editor. And we were back into revision. Ann polished our writing.

Thank you to Sue Stevenson for the back cover photo, Pat Richard for the Prudence Island map, East Bay Printers for their prompt and efficient printing service, and Korey Goulet—Horace M. Barrett's granddaughter—who photographed Horace's illustrations to complement our stories in *Home At Last*.